Stories
from

DATE DUE

Stories
from
Ancient Canaan

edited and translated
by Michael David Coogan

The Westminster Press
Philadelphia

First edition

PUBLISHED BY THE WESTMINSTER PRESS®
Philadelphia, Pennsylvania

Printed in the United States of America

9 8 7 6 5 4 3 2 1

For Liza

Library of Congress in Publication Data

Main entry under title:

Stories from ancient Canaan.

    Includes bibliographical references.
    CONTENTS: Introduction.—Aqhat.—The healers.—Kirta.—Baal.
    1. Ugaritic literature—Translations into English.
2. English literature—Translations from Ugaritic.
I. Coogan, Michael David.
PJ4150.Z95E5   1978   892'.6   77-20022
ISBN 0-664-24184-0

Contents

Preface

These translations were prompted by my experience in teaching an undergraduate course in ancient Near Eastern religions: while accurate, readable, and inexpensive versions of Mesopotamian and Egyptian religious literature are available, a similar edition of the principal Canaanite texts does not exist. This book is intended to fill that gap. It is written for the reader without linguistic or scholarly background, and should prove valuable for students of the history of religion, of the Bible, and of comparative literature.

Following general practice I have normalized most proper names to correspond to their biblical cognates.

My study of the language and literature of Ugarit began at Fordham University under George S. Glanzman, S.J., and continued under Frank Moore Cross at Harvard University. I am indebted to both of these extraordinary teachers, and if I have been able to communicate the substance and the spirit of this difficult material, it is in no small way due to the insights they shared with me.

The excerpts from *Enuma Elish* quoted on page 78 are taken from E. A. Speiser's translation in *Ancient Near Eastern Texts Relating to the Old Testament,* ed. by James B. Pritchard (Princeton, N.J.: Princeton University Press, 3d edition, 1969), pp. 61 and 64.

Introduction

" 'I have a word to tell you,
    a story to recount to you:
the word of the tree and the charm of the stone,
    the whisper of the heavens to the earth,
    of the seas to the stars.
I understand the lightning which the heavens do not know,
    the word which men do not know,
    and earth's masses cannot understand.
Come, and I will reveal it.' "

These lines were written more than thirty-four centuries
ago, when "the mystery sang alive still in the water and sing-
ing birds." In context they are part of an invitation from one
god to another; the god speaking is Baal, and the text in which
he is quoted comes from ancient Ugarit, a city destroyed by an
invasion of the Sea Peoples not long after 1200 B.C. and redis-
covered in 1928 by a Syrian plowman who accidentally opened
a tomb.

Ugarit, now called Ras Shamra (Cape Fennel), is located on
the north Syrian coast, and was one of the major Canaanite
city-states during the second millennium B.C. The cemetery of
Ugarit, with its vaulted tombs and painted pottery, at first suggested that the city was a Mycenaean colony, but as the first
texts were excavated, deciphered, and translated, it became
clear that Ugarit was Semitic. There were Mycenaeans there,
but they were only part of a polyglot and cosmopolitan port that
included Hittites, Babylonians, Hurrians, and Egyptians as well
as the native Canaanites.

The designation Canaanite requires some explanation. A
group of Semitic peoples who during the Bronze Age occupied
most of what is today Syria, Lebanon, Israel, and Jordan, the
Canaanites were never organized into a single political unit;
nevertheless, the relatively independent city-states such as Uga-

rit, Byblos, Sidon, Tyre, Shechem, and Jerusalem had a common language and culture (with local idiosyncracies) which we call Canaanite. To give just one example, the same type of alphabetic cuneiform writing used in the texts translated here has also turned up at several sites in Palestine.

THE TABLETS

During the nearly continuous excavations conducted at Ugarit since 1929, thousands of texts have been found. They include diplomatic correspondence, legal records, remedies for horses' ailments, long lists of gods, offerings, supplies, and personnel, dictionaries of word equivalents in the various languages used in the city, and the oldest complete alphabet, with an order substantially the same as that of our own. The fifteen tablets translated in this book have a common origin—all were found in the library of the chief priest of Baal in the city's main temple complex—and a common scribe, Ilimilku from Shubbani. His clear, precise touch with reed on damp clay is unmistakable, and he occasionally signed his work. Ilimilku did not, of course, compose these myths: he copied them as they were dictated by the chief priest Attanu-Purlianni; both were subsidized by Niqmaddu II, king of Ugarit, who reigned from c. 1375 to c. 1345 B.C. No other surviving texts have these indications of authorship and sponsorship; those translated here thus form a portfolio of sorts, an introduction to the literature of the Canaanites of Ugarit that they themselves took special steps to preserve.

The first of the four stories presented here, *Aqhat*, was written on three tablets and tells the story of Aqhat, the son of Danel, from his conception to his death and its consequences. The three fragmentary tablets that contain *The Healers* are probably a sequel to *Aqhat*, and describe the visit of those beneficent underworld deities to Danel after his son's murder. The story of *Kirta*, also preserved on three tablets, is an account of that king's quest for an heir, his illness and recovery, and the revolt of his son. Finally, the *Baal* cycle, on six tablets, is the episodic presentation of the storm god's defeat of his enemies and his assumption of the kingship over gods and men.

Like most of the texts from Ugarit, these were written on clay tablets, generally the size of a modern octavo volume, which were then baked. Both sides of the tablets were inscribed with from one to four columns divided by vertical lines, each column containing about fifty lines of text written continuously without spacing according to meter or sense. The scribe only rarely put single or double horizontal dividing lines between the lines of the text in order to indicate paragraphs or endings of episodes or to separate rubrics from the text proper. Occasionally the title of a tablet was given at its beginning; thus, two of the three parts of *Kirta* begin with the note "Concerning Kirta"; similarly we find "Concerning Baal" and "Concerning Aqhat" once each. It is possible that such a cataloging device may have headed each of the major mythological tablets, but since the tops of the columns have usually broken off, we cannot be sure.

Although the date of the present copies is known, the age of the myths themselves is not. Most scholars agree that they could have been composed as much as two or three centuries before they were finally written down, having been transmitted orally until then.

As we have noted, the texts were found adjacent to the main temple at Ugarit. This religious provenance is no accident: these are not just good stories; most of them must also have functioned, or originated, as librettos for actual rituals. But the stage directions to accompany the librettos were, if written down at all, kept separately, suggesting that for Ilimilku and Attanu-Purlianni, at least, the myths had independent value.

THE GODS OF UGARIT

Many of the protagonists in the stories contained in this collection are divine, but the myths and epics transcribed by Ilimilku are only one source of information about the Ugaritic pantheon. Other texts, especially ritual ones, as well as architectural remains and cultic art, add substantially to our knowledge, and a brief introduction to the gods and goddesses of Ugarit that draws on all sources may be helpful for the reader.

The head of the pantheon was El, as his epithets "the King" and "the Father of Gods" indicate. In the lists of deities and of the offerings made to them, El generally precedes the other major gods, although he himself can be preceded by "the older gods," the generation of predecessors he had presumably supplanted before the period of Ugarit's zenith. El's name is a common noun meaning "god"; its precise etymology is uncertain: the two major theories derive it from roots meaning "strong" or "first." In his role as head of the pantheon, El is well attested throughout the Semitic world. Compare, for example, the Arabic cognate Allah, which literally means "the god" or simply "God"; the epithets "the Merciful" and "the Kind" used of Allah are strikingly close to the Ugaritic designations of El as "the Kind, the Compassionate." The home of El, "the Creator of All," is a mountain from whose base issue the two rivers that are the source of all fresh water in the world. There he lives in a tent, and there the sons of El, the divine Assembly over which he presides, meet. In Ugaritic art El is depicted as a bearded patriarchal figure, although his behavior at a drinking feast (as described in a tablet not translated here) is hardly dignified.

One of the problems connected with El is the difficulty of assessing his importance in Ugaritic religion. It seems that by the time *Baal* was composed, El's position among the gods was ceremonial and without power. The attribution of kingship to Baal supports this view: Baal boasts, "I alone will rule over the gods," and this claim is echoed by both Anat and Asherah. Furthermore, it is noteworthy that no temple of El has yet been discovered at Ugarit, although the site has not been entirely excavated. Nevertheless, in the surviving Canaanite stories El is by no means an impotent ruler. It is he, and no other god, who can cure Kirta; it is he to whom Baal turns for help for Danel and of whom Anat asks permission to take revenge on Aqhat;

and, significantly, it is Baal, not El, who is vanquished by Death. The best explanation of these discrepancies is that Canaanite theology was not static. While El was the head of the pantheon, and actively so in earlier stories such as *Aqhat* and *Kirta,* Baal was becoming the dominant Canaanite deity, and the *Baal* cycle reflects this process.

Baal is the Ugaritic fertility god and the patron of the city, as his title, "Lord of Ugarit," shows. One of the two large temples discovered at Ras Shamra is dedicated to him, the other to his father Dagon, the god of grain. Baal's home is on Mount Zaphon, a high peak north of Ugarit and often visible from it. Mount Zaphon itself had divine status, as we learn from *Kirta:*

> "Baal's mountain, father, will weep for you,
>   Zaphon, the holy stronghold,
> the holy stronghold will lament,
>   the stronghold wide and broad."

Baal is depicted on a stele from Ras Shamra with a club in one hand and a lightning bolt in the other, and in the texts is often given the accouterments of a storm—clouds, wind, and rain. In the introduction to the *Baal* cycle we shall have occasion to study Baal's origin, character, and function more closely.

Three female deities appear regularly in the stories translated here—Anat, Asherah, and Astarte. None of them have major roles in the myths, for Ugaritic theology, like Ugaritic society, was patriarchal. Asherah is El's consort and hence the mother of the gods; she is sometimes identified with Astarte, the least mentioned of the three. The only goddess with a vivid character is Anat. She is Baal's wife and sister, and is closely identified with him as a source of fertility and a successful opponent of the forces of chaos; like Baal she lives on a mountain. Her fierce temper is directed against gods and mortals alike, and with her thirst for violence and her macabre trappings—a necklace of human heads, a belt of human hands—Anat has been compared to the Hindu goddess Kali.

The craftsman of the gods, Kothar-wa-Hasis, was thought to

live in distant lands, either Crete to the west or Egypt to the south. This reflects the Canaanites' dependence on foreign artisans for both inspiration and execution. Canaanite art is largely derivative, the most significant source of its motifs being Egypt; we have already noted the presence of Mycenaean painted pottery at Ugarit. Unlike his Greek counterpart Hephaistos, Kothar has no distinctive personality, but he is a master craftsman whose skill provides the gods, and occasionally chosen mortals, with weapons and palaces.

Finally we come to Death, Baal's adversary and antithesis, who personifies the forces of sterility and drought. The Syro-Palestinian landscape is divided into three general areas along its eastern and southern borders: the arable land gives way to semidesert, the territory where nomads pasture their flocks of sheep and goats, followed by the desert itself. This last is Death's domain, and the "desert pasture" in front of it is "Death's shore." His underworld home could be reached by raising the two mountains that block its entrance. The underworld is a damp, watery place called "the Swamp," "Muck," and "Phlegm." Another of its designations, "sanatorium," is the euphemistic title used for a leprosarium in II Kings 15:5.

As a group, the gods of the Canaanites are larger than life. They travel by giant strides—"a thousand fields, ten thousand acres at each step"—and their control over human destiny is absolute. They are personifications of realities beyond human understanding and control: the storms on which prosperity and even survival depended, the powerful drives of sex and violence, the final mystery of death. But they are also individuals belonging to a society that mirrors society on earth; the solutions of the problems of that "heavenly city" in their stories gave the Canaanites hope for the future.

POETRY AND LANGUAGE

The Canaanite dialect used at Ugarit is closely related to biblical Hebrew as well as to Phoenician, Aramaic, and Moabite. Like most ancient documents in those languages, it was written almost entirely without vowels, as are modern Hebrew and Arabic. This can complicate translation, since a word with three or four consonants may, at least theoretically, represent several grammatical forms.

Yet there is a compensating advantage for the translator of Ugaritic: the poetic techniques used by the ancient Canaanite authors have much in common with those employed in the Bible and in the *Iliad* and the *Odyssey*. As in biblical poetry, the chief formal characteristic of Canaanite verse is the use of parallelism, a characteristic not lost in translation. In parallelistic verse a single idea is expressed in units of two or three lines (a bicolon or a tricolon) by repetition, synonyms, or antonyms. Thus, the lines:

> "Let me tell you, Prince Baal,
> > let me repeat, Rider on the Clouds:
> behold, your enemy, Baal,
> > behold, you will kill your enemy,
> > behold, you will annihilate your foes.
> You will take your eternal kingship,
> > your dominion forever and ever"

consist of a tricolon framed by two bicola; each unit has one thought which is developed by repetitive and synonymous parallelism. Not only the technique but the lines themselves are familiar:

> Behold, your enemies, Yahweh,
> > behold, your enemies have perished,
> all evildoers have been scattered.
> > > > (Psalm 92:9)

> Your kingdom is an eternal kingdom,
> > your rule is forever and ever.
> > > > (Psalm 145:13)

This coincidence of style and formula is not surprising given the common tradition of the Canaanite and Israelite poets: the cultural continuum of ancient Canaan, stretching from northern Syria to southern Palestine, included not only material objects and language but religious and literary expression as well.

The extensive use of parallelism also clarifies obscurities. Many words in Ugaritic have no apparent cognates in other Semitic languages, and their precise meaning is therefore unknown; synonymous parallelism often provides a possible or even a probable sense. Nevertheless, to a literal-minded reader synonymous parallelism may cause some puzzlement. Thus, the divine command to Kirta:

> "Take a lamb in your hand,
>   a sacrificial lamb in your right hand,
>   a young animal in both your hands"

might seem to mean that the hero is to handle three animals at once. But the parallelism is impressionistic, not cumulative, and only one lamb is in question.

The use of numbers in parallelism may also be confusing. The synonym for any number (x) is the next higher unit (x + 1). The favorite numbers used in this way are three and four, seven and eight, and one thousand and ten thousand; ten thousand is the next unit after one thousand, as in English the next unit after a dozen is a gross. Extended use of this technique is found in Proverbs 30:18–31 and Amos 1:3 to 2:8, and individual examples in both Ugaritic and biblical poetry are too numerous to catalog here.

Also characteristic of Canaanite poetry is the repetitive use of epithets and of formulae describing typical actions; these techniques are Homeric as well. Thus, Baal is often called "the Rider on the Clouds" (compare the designation of Zeus as "the Cloud-gatherer"), or "the son of Dagon"—patronymics are common in the Greek as well as in the Canaanite epics. Sea, one of Baal's enemies, is given the parallel titles "Prince Sea" and "Judge River"; El is "the Kind, the Compassionate," "the Bull," "the Father of Time," and "the Father of Men" (see *Odyssey* I.28); Danel is regularly described as "the Healer's man," "the Hero," and "the man of the god of Harnam"; and so forth. There are standard descriptions of banquets and journeys, of the saddling of an ass, the offering of a sacrifice, and the arrival of a deity at El's home, to give just a few examples. These repeated formulae may strike us as clichés, but we should recall that ancient audiences, whether Greek or Canaanite, listened rather than read; repetition allowed for a lessening of attention at periodic intervals in the course of the narrative.

There are also common motifs, one of which is the measurement of time in periods of seven days or seven years. This usage occurs five times in *Aqhat* as well as elsewhere in the stories translated here, and is a pattern whose precise significance is still not known. One application of the seven-year formula is to alternating periods of plenty and famine, as in the dream of Pharaoh in the biblical story of Joseph (Genesis 41:26ff.); the motif is also found in Egyptian and Mesopotamian sources. In our texts, Baal's victory over Death extended for seven years during which the land was productive; throughout a corresponding seven-year cycle the forces of sterility prevailed over the storm god, as Danel's curse implies:

> "For seven years let Baal fail,
>   eight, the Rider on the Clouds:
> no dew, no showers,
>   no surging of the two seas,
>   no benefit of Baal's voice."

For the alternation of famine and plenty the entire seven-year period was significant; in other instances the emphasis is on the seventh day or year. Thus, it was on the seventh day of Danel's incubation rite in the temple that Baal interceded for him and El blessed him, just as it was on the seventh day that God called to Moses on the cloud-covered mountain (Exodus 24:16). Similarly, only on the seventh day of the Wise Women's ritual in *Aqhat* did Danel's impotence end; one of the themes of the first account of the Creation in the Bible is the importance of the seventh day, the Sabbath; and, in a final parade example, the fall of Jericho occurred on the seventh day after seven priests with seven trumpets marched seven times around the city (Joshua 6:15ff.).

Seven days is the standard length of a journey (*Kirta* I; Genesis 31:23) and of a wedding feast (Judges 14:12); the firing of Baal's palace takes a week as well. In these and other examples it is difficult to see more than literary convention in the choice of seven. But the alteration of the traditional mourning period from seven days (as in Job 2:13) to seven years after Aqhat's murder heightens the connections between Danel's son and the powers of fertility. Thus, in some cases we can agree with the observation that the seven-year period is "a time of great potency and fateful in its meaning" (H.-J. Kraus, *Worship in Israel: A Cultic History of the Old Testament* [Oxford: Basil Backwell; Richmond, Va.: John Knox Press, 1966]).

As this examination of parallelism, epithets, and formulae illustrates, ancient Semitic poets, whether Ugaritic or Israelite, were conservative. Traditional techniques and motifs were preserved, with modifications, for at least a millennium. But the Israelites' indebtedness to their Canaanite predecessors was not merely linguistic and literary, as we shall now observe.

UGARIT AND ISRAEL

Until the discovery of Ugarit, the sources for the study of the religion of ancient Canaan were both sketchy and late. There were distorted and fragmentary accounts in the classical authors and in some early Christian apologists; there were also dedicatory and funerary inscriptions of the Phoenicians and their western Punic cousins. But even when one considered this literary evidence in the context of the archaeological remains—the figurines and statues, the temples and shrines—it was impossible to reconstruct a coherent account of what the Canaanites believed.

The Bible contains many direct references to Canaanite religious practice and ideology, but not surprisingly they are almost uniformly hostile and are thus presumably distorted. Now, with

the discovery of Ugarit and its thousands of texts, we have an
extensive and primary source for the study of Canaanite religion, and with it we can reinterpret the biblical evidence concerning the Canaanites. At the same time we can deepen our
understanding of the Law, the Prophets, and the Writings, for
the Ugaritic tablets are the best available witness to the background from which the religion of Israel emerged, and to the
Canaanite beliefs that it shared, adopted, compromised with,
and sometimes rejected.

Perhaps the best way to illumine this relationship between
Israel and Ugarit is to return to the principal Canaanite divini-
ties and to examine their biblical analogues. The head of the
pantheon, El, also appears in the Bible. His name (and its variant Elohim) is generally used as a term for god, but in a few
passages it must be a proper name. Thus, Psalm 82 begins:

> God [Elohim] has taken his place in the
>   Assembly of El,
>   in the midst of the gods [elohim] he
>   holds judgment.

Similarly, Isaiah 14:13 (although in a polemical context) speaks
of the "stars of El," and Deuteronomy 32:8 (following the read-
ing of a Dead Sea scroll and the Greek text) of the "sons of El."
In Exodus 6:2–3 a distinction is made between earlier and later
names of the god of Israel:

> God [Elohim] spoke to Moses, and he said to him: "I am Yahweh.
> I appeared to Abraham, Isaac, and Jacob as El Shadday, but by my
> name Yahweh I was not known to them."

The title El Shadday, often erroneously translated "God Al-
mighty," means "El of the Mountain," or "El, the One of the
Mountain." As we have seen, El lived on a mountain, the "cosmic mountain" that was the source of fresh water and the seat
of the divine Assembly, and the biblical epithet reflects this
mythology.

Other titles of El in the Bible also echo Ugaritic formulae.

Thus, in Genesis 21:33, Yahweh is styled "El, the Eternal One," reminding us of El's title, "the Father of Time"; the phrase "the Mighty One of Jacob" (Genesis 49:24; etc.) should probably be rendered "the Bull of Jacob," recalling El's identification as "the Bull"; and the liturgical phrase, "Yahweh, Yahweh, a merciful and gracious god [*el*], slow to anger and quick to forgive," (Exodus 34:6; etc.) is a variant of "El the Kind, the Compassionate."

The popularity of the worship of Baal in Israel is illustrated both by the prophets' repeated attacks on it and by the use of Baal as an element in personal names; among others, Saul and even David gave their children names containing Baal (an example is Baalyada, meaning "Baal knows"). One reason for Baalism's appeal for the Israelites and the consequent syncretistic identification of Yahweh with Baal is that many of Yahweh's characteristics and much of the language used to describe him were derived from his Canaanite rival. Both are called "Rider on the Clouds" (Yahweh in Psalm 68:4), and some commentators have suggested that Psalm 29 was originally a hymn to Baal; its language is in any case strikingly familiar to a reader of the *Baal* cycle. Like Baal, Yahweh was the victorious warrior who had shown his mastery over the sea; like Baal, Yahweh revealed himself on a mountain in the midst of a storm; like Baal, Yahweh had a temple built of cedar.

The character of the god of Israel is thus a composite; while Yahweh is primarily an El figure, many of the images and formulae that distinguish him from El are adopted from the theology of Baal. It is significant that the revelation of the name of Yahweh, symbolizing a dramatic change in Israel's understanding of and relationship with her god, is set in the period of the Exodus and Conquest. For it was when Israel made the transition from a (semi)nomadic to a sedentary and eventually urban way of life that it passed from the milieu of the patriarchs who worshiped El, a patriarchal tent dweller, to the world of the Canaanite city-states and kingdoms, whose chief divinity was Baal, young, active, and living in a house.

Let us examine more closely the motif of the mountain where Yahweh revealed himself. The primary mountain of revelation was Sinai; when Yahweh appeared,

> there was thunder and lightning and a heavy cloud on the mountain. . . . And Mount Sinai was covered with smoke, because Yahweh had descended upon it in fire. . . . And the whole mountain quaked violently. (Exodus 19:16–18)

The same imagery is used of Baal's theophany:

> Then Baal opened a slit in the clouds,
> Baal sounded his holy voice,
> Baal thundered from his lips . . .
> the earth's high places shook.

The association of Yahweh as storm god with the mountain of revelation is echoed in Judges 5:4–5:

> Yahweh, when you set out from Seir,
> when you marched from the field of Edom,
> the earth quaked,
> and the heavens shook,
> and the clouds shook water;
> the mountains shuddered before Yahweh, the one
> of Sinai,
> before Yahweh, the god of Israel.

The other mountain central to Israel's theology was Mount Zion. Jerusalem had been a center of El worship, as Genesis 14.18–24 illustrates: there Melchizedek was a priest of El Most High (El Elyon). Like the mountain of El in the Ugaritic texts, Zion was (at least in apocalyptic vision) the source of fresh water:

> On that day living waters will go out from Jerusalem, half of them to the eastern sea, half of them to the western sea, both in summer and in winter. (Zechariah 14:8)

This theme recurs in Ezekiel 47:1–12, Joel 3:17–18, and Revelation 22:1–2.

But just as elements of the cults of El and Baal blended in
the worship of Yahweh, so too Zion and Sinai became confused:

> Out of Zion, perfect in beauty,
>   God shines forth. . . .
> before him is a consuming fire,
>   around him a storm rages.
>
> (Psalm 50:2–3)

And as Zion assumed the characteristics of the storm god's
home, it inevitably became identified with it:

> His holy mountain, beautiful in elevation,
>   is the joy of the whole earth;
> Mount Zion, in the recesses of Zaphon,
>   is the city of the great king.
>
> (Psalm 48:2–3)

Turning now to the other deities, we find traces of Anat,
Asherah, and Astarte in the Bible. Anat is the least well attested,
occurring only in the place-names Beth-Anath and Anathoth
and in the personal name Shamgar Ben-Anath. One reason for
Anat's apparent decline may have been the transfer of El's wife
Asherah to Baal. It has been suggested that Asherah's close
association with Baal in the Bible (see, for example, I Kings
18:19) may indicate that she had become his wife. If this is
correct, the process of Baal's replacement of El was complete,
for possession of the king's wife was a visible sign of power; both
Absalom and Adonijah realized that the physical (and, in Absalom's case, public) possession of David's concubines would
demonstrate their father's weakness and enhance their own
claims to the kingship. In biblical Hebrew the word Asherah is
also a common noun, meaning a sacred tree or pole used in the
goddess's cult that was probably a fertility symbol; again,
Asherah is implicitly associated with Baal, the fertility god *par
excellence*. Astarte occurs in the Bible with some frequency,
but, as in extant Ugaritic sources, little light is shed on her
personality. She is called "the goddess" or "the abomination of
the Sidonians."

As a deity, Death is seldom mentioned in the Bible. As in the Ugaritic texts, his appetite is proverbial, and his underworld domain is a watery place:

> The waters engulfed me up to my neck,
> the sea surrounded me;
> reeds were wound on my head
> at the roots of the mountains.
>
> (Jonah 2:5-6)

In Isaiah 25:8 it is said that at the eschatological victory banquet Yahweh "will swallow up Death forever"; this is a reversal of the scene in *Baal* when the storm god goes down into Death's mouth, to be crushed like a kid in his jaws.

As this brief overview has shown, Canaanite motifs are ubiquitous in the Bible. Most significant is the fusion of Baal-language and El-language in the descriptions of Yahweh and his activity: the god of Israel may be unique, but the formulae with which Israel expressed her understanding of him were not. The more we learn of the cultural context in which the Israelites lived, the more the prophetic remark rings true:

> By origin and by birth you are of the land of the Canaanites.
>
> (Ezekiel 16:3)

A NOTE ON THIS TRANSLATION

My intention has been to let the texts speak for themselves by providing a readable translation unencumbered by the usual scholarly apparatus and commentary. I have therefore thought it unnecessary to signal all omissions and reconstructions. Nevertheless, because of the fragmentary state of most of the tablets, it has been unavoidable to use three spaced periods to indicate a gap of several words, and a full line of spaced periods to indicate a more substantial break.

For the reader's convenience I have included a glossary of most proper names and titles appearing in the stories. More detailed expositions of the myths and their principal characters can be found in the readings suggested below.

SUGGESTIONS FOR FURTHER READING

A succinct summary, with a bibliography, of the history and literature of Ugarit is Margaret S. Drower's "Ugarit," Ch. XXI (b) of *The Cambridge Ancient History,* Vol. II, Part II (Cambridge: Cambridge University Press, 3d ed., 1975). In his study *Religions of the Ancient Near East* (London: S.P.C.K.; Philadelphia: The Westminster Press, 1973), Helmer Ringgren has devoted a chapter to the religious aspects of the Ugaritic texts. More detailed and occasionally tangential treatments may be found in the following:

William Foxwell Albright, *Yahweh and the Gods of Canaan* (London: The Athlone Press; Garden City, N.Y.: Doubleday & Co., Inc., 1968), especially Ch. III, "Canaanite Religion in the Bronze Age"; and *Archaeology and the Religion of Israel* (Garden City, N.Y.: Doubleday & Co., 5th ed., 1969), especially Ch. III, "Archaeology and the Religion of the Canaanites."

Umberto Cassuto, *The Goddess Anath: Canaanite Epics of the Patriarchal Age* (Jerusalem: The Magnes Press, The Hebrew University, 1971).

Richard J. Clifford, *The Cosmic Mountain in Canaan and the Old Testament* (Cambridge, Mass.: Harvard University Press, 1972).

Frank Moore Cross, *Canaanite Myth and Hebrew Epic: Essays in the History of the Religion of Israel* (Cambridge, Mass.: Harvard University Press, 1973).

Mitchell J. Dahood, "Ancient Semitic Deities in Syria and Palestine," pp. 65–94 in *Le antiche divinità semitiche,* ed. by Sabatino Moscati (Rome: Centro di Studi Semitici, University of Rome, 1958).

John Gray, *The Legacy of Canaan: The Ras Shamra Texts and Their Relevance to the Old Testament* (Leiden: E. J. Brill, 2d ed., 1965).

Arvid S. Kapelrud, *Baal in the Ras Shamra Texts* (Copenhagen: G. E. C. Gad, 1952), and *The Violent Goddess: Anat in the Ras Shamra Texts* (Oslo: Universitetsforlaget, 1969).

Patrick D. Miller, Jr., *The Divine Warrior in Early Israel* (Cambridge, Mass.: Harvard University Press, 1973).

Marvin H. Pope, *El in the Ugaritic Texts* (Leiden: E. J. Brill, 1955).
The annual *Ugarit-Forschungen* (Neukirchen-Vluyn: Neukirchener Verlag, 1969–) contains technical articles in French, German, and English on all aspects of the Ugaritic material.

A NOTE ON SOURCES

The standard critical edition of the alphabetic texts from Ras Shamra is Andrée Herdner's *Corpus des tablettes en cunéiformes alphabétiques découvertes à Ras Shamra-Ugarit de 1929 à 1939* (two volumes; Paris: Imprimerie Nationale, 1963); there is a full bibliography for each text. Of the texts translated here, *Baal* is Nos. 1 to 6 in Herdner's edition, *Kirta* is Nos. 14 to 16, *Aqhat* is Nos. 17 to 19, and *The Healers* is Nos. 20 to 22.

A convenient grammar and glossary together with transcriptions of all the texts (including some not contained in Herdner's edition, since they were found after 1939) is Cyrus H. Gordon's *Ugaritic Textbook* (three volumes; Rome: Pontifical Biblical Institute, 1965).

The following five critical translations of the Canaanite myths and epics have been of invaluable help in the preparation of my own. If I have disagreed with them at some points it is only because "the dwarf sees farther than the giant, when he has the giant's shoulder to mount on."

André Caquot, Maurice Sznycer, and Andrée Herdner, *Textes ougaritiques. I. Mythes et légendes (Littératures anciennes du Proche-Orient,* Vol. 7; Paris: Les Éditions du Cerf, 1974).
Godfrey Rolles Driver, *Canaanite Myths and Legends* (Edinburgh: T. & T. Clark, 1956).
Theodor H. Gaster, *Thespis: Ritual, Myth and Drama in the Ancient Near East* (Staten Island, N.Y.: Gordian Press, Inc., 2d ed., 1975).
H. L. Ginsberg, "Ugaritic Myths, Epics, and Legends," pp. 129–155 in *Ancient Near Eastern Texts Relating to the Old Testament,* ed. by James B. Pritchard (Princeton, N.J.: Princeton University Press, 3d ed., 1969).
Cyrus H. Gordon, *Ugaritic Literature: A Comprehensive Translation of the Poetic and Prose Texts* (Rome: Pontifical Biblical Institute, 1949).

AQHAT

INTRODUCTION

"You are wiser than Danel,
no secret is hidden from you."
(Ezekiel 28:3)

With these words the sixth-century B.C. Israelite prophet
satirized his contemporary, the king of Tyre. The Danel or (as
traditionally pronounced) Daniel in question, also mentioned
together with Noah and Job in Ezekiel 14, was generally identified with the legendary hero of the Book of Daniel until the
discovery of the Ugaritic texts. But the spelling of the name in
the Hebrew text, its date, and its context make it clear that the
Danel referred to by Ezekiel is the Canaanite king, the father
of Aqhat.

The three fragmentary tablets from Ras Shamra that deal
with Danel and his son do not, unfortunately, illustrate his
proverbial wisdom; we must presume that other parts of the
cycle, as yet undiscovered, contained episodes similar to the
biblical passages that show Solomon to be the quintessentially
wise king. (See I Kings 3:16–28; 4:29–34; 10:1–10.) In a formulaic passage occurring twice in the surviving texts, Danel is
described as sitting at the entrance to the city gate, presiding
over legal cases involving widows and orphans. This was the
ordinary task of an Oriental monarch: by protecting the most
powerless members of society the king demonstrated his own
strength. The presentation of Danel as a judge is thus evidence
for his royal status, but does not imply unusual sagacity. Virtually the same formula is used, for example, by Hammurabi in
the epilogue to his famous Code and, in a negative sense, of
Kirta.

As the first tablet begins, Danel is described in a temple

performing an incubation rite. This was considered an effective way of communicating with a divine power, as biblical parallels involving Samuel and Solomon make clear. The specific reason for Danel's vigil is revealed when, on the seventh day, his patron god Baal interceded for him with El: Danel had no son and heir. The focus of the story from its beginning is thus on Danel's son and not on the king himself; this is confirmed by the title "Concerning Aqhat" at the beginning of the third tablet of the cycle. We learn later that Danel did have a daughter, Pagat, but for the ancient Canaanites (as well as in many modern societies) a son was the desired offspring. "Like arrows in the hands of a warrior are the sons of one's youth; happy is the man whose quiver is full of them." (Psalm 127:4–5.)

After a repeated catalog of the duties of a son, El, the head of the pantheon, promised that Danel would father one. Danel returned to his palace, where, with the accompanying ministrations of the goddesses of marriage and childbirth, a son was conceived. There is now a break amounting to about a third of the first tablet.

The story resumes with a visit of Kothar-wa-Hasis, the Canaanite Hephaistos, to Danel. In typical Oriental fashion a feast was prepared in his honor, and he presented Danel with a bow and arrows; Danel gave them to his son Aqhat. Weapons from the divine craftsman were wonderful objects—we are reminded of the shield of Achilles—and it is little surprise that Anat, the goddess of love and war, was envious of Aqhat. She offered him gold and silver for the bow and arrows, which he refused, and finally the ultimate gift, immortality. Aqhat rejected this bribe in less than conciliatory terms, asserting that despite the goddess's promises death awaited him, as it does every man; his skull would be plastered and put into a tomb. (Such plaster-covered skulls have been excavated at ancient Jericho.) He rashly went on to insult Anat, denying her pretensions to hunting ability.

The scene between Aqhat and Anat is reminiscent of one between the Mesopotamian hero Gilgamesh and the corresponding goddess of love and war Ishtar. In the Gilgamesh epic, a fragment of which has been found at Ugarit, the goddess attempted to seduce the hero, but he rejected her advances and added to the insult by listing her previous lovers and their unhappy fates. Like Anat, Ishtar complained to her father, the head of the pantheon; like Anat, she sought revenge by means of an animal. Furthermore, Anu, the father of the gods, warned Ishtar of the consequences of her revenge: "If I do what you ask, there will be seven years of barren husks"; similarly, a drought of seven years followed the death of Aqhat. These close parallels have prompted the suggestion that Anat was after more than Aqhat's bow, that the bow was a symbol of the hero's masculinity; but the larger context, including the bow's origin and its being dropped into the sea, makes the obvious sense the most likely one. We have here, nevertheless, a clear example of the interdependence of ancient Near Eastern literatures, of the way a common theme can be given variations. Greco-Roman mythology has other, though less obvious, examples of the same pattern.

With El, under duress, acquiescing to her desire for revenge, Anat proceeded to kill Aqhat through the agency of her henchman Yatpan. Both assumed the form of birds (we recall Athena's frequent appearances as a bird), and Yatpan descended upon Aqhat while he was eating: "He struck him twice on the skull, three times over the ear." The consequences of Aqhat's death were catastrophic: the crops immediately died. Vultures hovered over Danel's house, a sure sign of death. Even before they knew the identity of the dead person, Danel and his daughter Pagat began to mourn. Danel then toured his blasted fields, ironically wishing that Aqhat, still alive as far as he knew, could harvest the once abundant crops. On his return messengers brought the news of Aqhat's murder. Anxious to give his son a proper burial, Danel searched the innards of the vultures for undigested fat and bone, and, having found them, buried what was left of Aqhat. He then cursed the three cities near the scene of the crime and officially began the seven-year period of mourning. At its end, signaled by the offering of sacrifice, Pagat asked for her father's blessing so that she might avenge her brother's death.

The figure of Pagat is an attractive one. Three times she is described by the formula:

> She gets up early to draw water,
> she brushes the dew from the barley,
> she knows the course of the stars.

These expressions represent her as an industrious housegirl, rising before dawn, while the stars were still visible and before the heavy dew had evaporated, to fetch the day's water supply —an ancient Cinderella. To us this activity might seem unsuited to a king's daughter, but the ancient Semites thought otherwise; the "valiant woman" of Proverbs 31, even though mistress of a large household, similarly "rises while it is still night" to secure enough food for the day, and Kirta's daughter Thitmanit, also a princess, met her brother as she was on her way to draw water at dusk.

Like Judith, Pagat applied cosmetics and put on her robe— but under it she concealed a dagger. Having arrived at Yatpan's camp, she managed to get him drunk, and in his cups he boasted of his murder of Aqhat. The tablet breaks off here, but it is probable that Pagat eventually killed Yatpan, if we can rely on Canaanite and Egyptian parallels in which a sister avenged her brother's violent death. In *Baal* it was Anat herself who seized and dismembered Baal's adversary Death, scattering his remains in the fields. Similarly, in Egyptian myth, after Osiris was murdered by his brother Seth, the god of the desert, his wife and sister Isis retrieved his body, buried it, and aided their son Horus to avenge his father.

The coincidence of themes here—the deaths of Baal, Osiris, and Aqhat were threats to fertility, the bodies of Death, Osiris, and Aqhat were all dismembered—suggests one level of interpretation for *Aqhat* as a whole. Nearly every Ugaritic text translated here has to do with fertility in some way, and *Aqhat* is no exception. Just as Baal's subjection to Death resulted in drought, so a drought followed Aqhat's murder. As the fragmentary texts which we have called *The Healers* suggest, the Aqhat cycle presumably continued with his restoration to life and the consequent return of fertility to the fields. For the king and, by extension, his son were vital to continued agricultural prosperity. *Kirta* indicates this, for when Kirta the king became ill, the farmers noted that

> gone was the food from their bins,
> gone was the wine from their skins,
> gone was the oil from their vats.

But despite an obvious relationship to the themes of *Baal* and *Kirta,* the emphasis in *Aqhat* is not here. Rather, as far as we can judge from the fragmentary state of the tablets, we have a complex saga depicting life as it was in days gone by. Concern with fertility is part of this picture, but only part. In one scene after another, the virtuous king, the ideal son, the dutiful daughter, and the rash young prince are sketched as models or as a warning. And behind these portraits lies the world of the gods who dealt with men face to face in those days—often capriciously, but with important consequences. As we have suggested, we do not know in what context *Aqhat* was recited at Ugarit. Perhaps by the time it was dictated by Attanu-Purlianni and transcribed by Ilimilku the cycle had no real function, cultic or otherwise, but was simply literature for its own sake, preserved because it was, in the end, a good story.

AQHAT

I

Then Danel, the Healer's man,
    the Hero, the man of the god of Harnam,
made an offering for the gods to eat,
    made an offering for the holy ones to drink.
Then he climbed onto his mat and lay down,
    onto his pallet, where he spent the night.
One day had ended, and on the second
Danel made an offering to the gods,
    an offering for the gods to eat,
    an offering for the holy ones to drink.
Three days had ended, and on the fourth
Danel made an offering to the gods,
    an offering for the gods to eat,
    an offering for the holy ones to drink.
Five days had ended, and on the sixth
Danel made an offering to the gods,
    an offering for the gods to eat,
    an offering for the holy ones to drink.
Danel climbed onto his mat,
    he climbed onto his mat and lay down,
    onto his pallet, where he spent the night.
Then, on the seventh day,
Baal approached the Assembly with his plea:
"Danel, the Healer's man, is unhappy;
    the Hero, the man of the god of Harnam, sighs:
he has no son, but his brothers do,
    no heir, like his cousins;
unlike his brothers, he has no son,
    nor an heir, like his cousins.
Yet he has made an offering for the gods to eat,

an offering for the holy ones to drink.
So, my father, El the Bull, won't you bless him?
    Creator of All, won't you show him your favor?
Let him have a son in his house,
    a descendant inside his palace,
to set up a stele for his divine ancestor,
    a family shrine in the sanctuary;
to free his spirit from the earth,
    guard his footsteps from the Slime;
to crush those who rebel against him,
    drive off his oppressors;
to hold his hand when he is drunk,
    support him when he is full of wine;
to eat his offering in the temple of Baal,
    his portion in the temple of El;
to patch his roof when it leaks,
    wash his clothes when they are dirty."
El took care of his servant,
    he blessed Danel, the Healer's man,
    he showed favor to the Hero, the man of the god of
        Harnam:
"Let the passion of Danel, the Healer's man, revive,
    the desire of the Hero, the man of the god of Harnam.
Let him go up to his bed:
when he kisses his wife she'll become pregnant;
    when he embraces her she'll conceive:
she will become pregnant, she will give birth, she will
        conceive;
and there will be a son in his house,
    an heir inside his palace,
to set up a stele for his divine ancestor,
    a family shrine in the sanctuary;
to free his spirit from the earth,
    guard his footsteps from the Slime;
to crush those who rebel against him,
    drive off his oppressors. . . ."

. . . .
". . . a family shrine in the sanctuary;
to free your spirit from the earth,
    guard your footsteps from the Slime;
to crush those who rebel against you,
    drive off your oppressors;
to eat your offering in the temple of Baal,
    your portion in the temple of El;
to hold your hand when you are drunk,
    support you when you are full of wine;
to patch your roof when it leaks,
    wash your clothes when they are dirty."
Danel's face was glad,
    and above his brow shone.
He opened his mouth and laughed,
    put his feet on a stool,
    raised his voice and shouted:
"Now I can sit back and relax;
    my heart inside me can relax;
for a son will be born to me, like my brothers,
    an heir, like my cousins,
who will set up a stele for my divine ancestor,
    a family shrine in the sanctuary;
who will free my spirit from the earth,
    guard my footsteps from the Slime;
who will crush those who rebel against me,
    drive off my oppressors;
who will hold my hand when I am drunk,
    support me when I am full of wine;
who will eat my offering in the temple of Baal,
    my portion in the temple of El;
who will patch my roof when it leaks,
    wash my clothes when they are dirty."
Danel arrived at his house,
    Danel reached his palace.
The Wise Women entered his house,

the Singers, the Swallows.
Then Danel, the Healer's man,
    the Hero, the man of the god of Harnam,
slaughtered an ox for the Wise Women,
    he gave food to the Wise Women,
    drink to the Singers, the Swallows.
One day had ended, and on the second
he gave food to the Wise Women,
    drink to the Singers, the Swallows.
Three days had ended, and on the fourth
he gave food to the Wise Women,
    drink to the Singers, the Swallows.
Five days had ended, and on the sixth
he gave food to the Wise Women,
    drink to the Singers, the Swallows.
Then, on the seventh day,
the Wise Women left his house,
    the Singers, the Swallows . . . .
. . . the pleasures of bed,
. . . the delights of bed . . . .
Danel sat and counted the months.
. . . .
"I'll bring a bow there,
    I'll provide the arrows."
And then, on the seventh day,
Danel, the Healer's man,
    the Hero, the man of the god of Harnam,
got up and sat at the entrance to the gate,
    next to the granary on the threshing floor.
He judged the cases of widows,
    presided over orphans' hearings.
Then he raised his eyes and looked:
    a thousand fields, ten thousand acres at each step,
he saw Kothar coming,
    he saw Hasis approaching;
not only was he bringing a bow,

he had also provided arrows.
Then Danel, the Healer's man,
     the Hero, the man of the god of Harnam,
called to his wife:
"Listen, Lady Danataya:
     prepare a lamb from the flock
for Kothar-wa-Hasis' appetite,
     for the desire of the Clever Craftsman.
Give food and drink to the god;
     serve and honor him,
     the lord of Egypt, the god of it all."
Lady Danataya obeyed;
     she prepared a lamb from the flock
for Kothar-wa-Hasis' appetite,
     for the desire of the Clever Craftsman.
After Kothar-wa-Hasis had arrived,
     he put the bow in Danel's hands,
     he set the arrows on his knees.
Then Lady Danataya gave food and drink to the god;
     she served and honored him,
     the lord of Egypt, the god of it all.
Kothar left for his tent,
     the Clever One for his divine home.

. . . .

Anat poured her cup on the ground,
     she raised her voice and shouted:
"Listen, Aqhat the Hero:
if you want silver, I'll give it to you,
     or gold—I'll make it yours.
But give your bow to Anat,
     let the Mistress of the Peoples have your arrows."
But Aqhat the Hero replied:
"I'll donate wood from the Lebanon,
     I'll donate tendons from wild oxen,
I'll donate horns from mountain goats,
     sinews from the hocks of a bull,

I'll donate reeds from the vast marshes;
    give them to Kothar-wa-Hasis:
he'll make a bow for Anat,
    arrows for the Mistress of the Peoples."
But the Virgin Anat replied:
"If you want eternal life, Aqhat the Hero,
    even if you want eternal life, I'll give it to you,
    immortality—I'll make it yours.
You'll be able to match years with Baal,
    months with the sons of El.
For when Baal gives life, he makes a feast,
    makes a feast for the life-given and gives him drinks;
he sings a song in his honor,
    a pleasant refrain for him.
So will I give life to Aqhat the Hero."
But Aqhat the Hero replied:
"Don't lie to me, Virgin,
    for with a hero your lies are wasted.
A mortal—what does he get in the end?
    what does a mortal finally get?
plaster poured on his head,
    lime on top of his skull.
As every man dies, I will die;
    yes, I too will surely die.
And I have something else to tell you:
bows are for men!
    Do women ever hunt?"
Anat laughed, but not in her heart;
    she replied:
"Listen to me, Aqhat the Hero,
    listen to me while I speak:
I'll surely meet you on the path of rebellion,
    on the proud path I'll make you fall
    under my feet, pretty-boy, he-man."
She stamped her feet and left the earth;
    then she headed toward El,

at the source of the two rivers,
    in the midst of the two seas' pools;
she opened El's tent and entered
    the shrine of the King, the Father of Time.
At El's feet she bowed down and adored,
    she prostrated herself and worshiped him.
Then she maligned Aqhat the Hero,
    she slandered the child of Danel, the Healer's man.

. . . .

II

. . . .

And the Virgin Anat replied:
"Don't rejoice in your well-built house,
    in your well-built house, El,
don't rejoice in the height of your palace:
    don't rely on them!
I'll smash your head,
    I'll make your gray hair run with blood,
    your gray beard with gore;
then you may call to Aqhat—he can save you;
    to the son of Danel—he can save you
    from the hand of the Virgin Anat!"
But El the Kind, the Compassionate, replied:
"I know you, daughter, how gentle you can be;
    but there is no restraint among goddesses.
Leave, my unscrupulous daughter;
    you will store it up in your heart,
and then whatever you desire you will do,
    whatever you wish;
    whoever slanders you will be crushed."
The Virgin Anat left;
    she headed toward Aqhat the Hero,
    a thousand fields, ten thousand acres at each step.
And the Virgin Anat laughed;

    she raised her voice and shouted:
"Listen, Aqhat the Hero:
    you are my brother and I am your sister. . . ."
. . . .
The Virgin Anat left,
    she headed for Yatpan, the Lady's man.
She raised her voice and shouted:
"Pay attention, Yatpan:
Aqhat is now in the city of Abiluma,
    Abiluma, the city of Prince Moon. . . ."
But Yatpan, the Lady's man, replied:
"Listen, Virgin Anat:
will you really kill him for his bow,
    kill him for his arrows,
    not let him live?
Pretty-boy, the Hero, has fixed a meal;
    he is all alone in the pavilion."
But the Virgin Anat replied:
"Pay attention, Yatpan, and I'll give the orders.
I'll put you in my pouch like a vulture,
    in my bag like a bird.
When Aqhat sits down to eat,
    the son of Danel to his meal,
vultures will swoop over him,
    a flock of birds will soar above.
I'll be swooping among the vultures,
    I'll set you over Aqhat:
strike him twice on the skull,
    three times over the ear;
make his blood run like a slaughterer,
    run to his knees like a butcher.
His breath will leave him like wind,
    his spirit like a breeze,
    like smoke from his nostrils;
his strength will leave his nostrils.
I won't let him live!"

She took Yatpan, the Lady's man,
    she put him in her pouch like a vulture,
    in her bag like a bird.
When Aqhat sat down to eat,
    the son of Danel to his meal,
vultures swooped over him,
    a flock of birds soared above.
Among the vultures swooped Anat;
    she set him over Aqhat.
He struck him twice on the skull,
    three times over the ear;
he made his blood run like a slaughterer,
    run to his knees like a butcher.
His breath left him like wind,
    his spirit like a breeze,
    like smoke from his nostrils. . . .
And she wept.

. . . .

III

. . . into the water it fell . . .
    the bow was broken.

. . . .

"I killed him only for his bow,
    I killed him for his arrows;
I did not let him live,
    but his bow has not become mine.
And because of his death
    the first fruits of summer have withered,
    the ear in its husk.

. . . .

Then Danel, the Healer's man,
    the Hero, the man of the god of Harnam,
got up and sat at the entrance to the gate,
    next to the granary on the threshing floor.

He judged the cases of widows,
  presided over orphans' hearings. . . .
Pagat raised her eyes and looked:
on the threshing floor the greenery had dried,
  it drooped, it had withered.
Over her father's house vultures were swooping,
  a flock of birds soared above.
Pagat wept in her heart,
  she cried inwardly.
She tore the clothes of Danel, the Healer's man,
  the garments of the Hero, the man of the god of
    Harnam.
Then Danel, the Healer's man,
cursed the clouds in the still heat,
  the rain of the clouds which falls in summer,
  the dew which drops on the grapes:
"For seven years let Baal fail,
  eight, the Rider on the Clouds:
no dew, no showers,
  no surging of the two seas,
  no benefit of Baal's voice.
For the clothes of Danel, the Healer's man, have been torn,
  the garments of the Hero, the man of the god of
    Harnam."
Danel called to his daughter:
"Listen, Pagat,
you get up early to draw water,
  you brush the dew from the barley,
  you know the course of the stars.
Saddle an ass, harness a donkey;
  attach my silver reins, my golden bridle."
Pagat obeyed,
she who got up early to draw water,
  who brushed the dew from the barley,
  who knew the course of the stars;
in tears she saddled the ass,

in tears she harnessed the donkey,
in tears she lifted her father,
she put him on the ass's back,
on the splendid back of the donkey.
Danel made a tour of inspection in his fields;
he saw a stalk in the fields,
he saw a stalk in the plots;
he embraced the stalk and kissed it:
"If only the stalk could grow,
in the fields the stalk grow,
in the plots the plant,
the hand of Aqhat the Hero would harvest you,
place you in the granary."
He made a tour of inspection in his plots;
he saw an ear growing in the plots,
an ear growing in the scorched fields.
He embraced the ear and kissed it:
"If only the ear could grow,
in the plots the ear grow,
in the scorched fields the plant,
the hand of Aqhat the Hero would harvest you,
place you in the granary."
These words had just come from his mouth,
this speech from his lips,
when she raised her eyes and looked:
two lads were coming. . . .
"He was struck twice on the skull,
three times over the ear. . . ."
Tears poured like quarter-shekels. . . .
"We have news for you, Danel. . . .
She made his breath leave him like wind,
his spirit like a breeze,
like smoke from his nostrils."
They arrived; they raised their voices and shouted:
"Listen, Danel, the Healer's man:
Aqhat the Hero is dead.

The Virgin Anat made his breath leave him like wind,
    his spirit like a breeze."
His feet shook,
    his face broke out in sweat,
    his back was as though shattered,
    his joints trembled,
    his vertebrae weakened.
. . . .
When he raised his eyes and looked,
    he saw vultures in the clouds.
He raised his voice and shouted:
"May Baal shatter the vultures' wings,
    may Baal shatter their pinions;
    let them fall at my feet.
I will split their gizzards and look;
    if there is fat, if there is bone,
I will weep and I will bury him,
    I will put him into the hole of the gods of the earth."
These words had just come from his mouth,
    this speech from his lips,
when Baal shattered the vultures' wings,
    Baal shattered their pinions,
    and they fell at his feet.
He split their gizzards and looked;
    there was no fat, there was no bone.
He raised his voice and shouted:
"May Baal rebuild the vultures' wings,
    may Baal rebuild their pinions;
vultures, up, and fly away!"
When he raised his eyes and looked,
    he saw Hirgab, the father of vultures.
He raised his voice and shouted:
"May Baal shatter Hirgab's wings,
    may Baal shatter his pinions:
    let him fall at my feet.
I will split his gizzard and look;

if there is fat, if there is bone,
I will weep and I will bury him,
   I will put him into the hole of the gods of the earth."
These words had just come from his mouth,
   this speech from his lips,
when Baal shattered Hirgab's wings,
   Baal shattered his pinions,
   and he fell at his feet.
He split his gizzard and looked;
   there was no fat, there was no bone.
He raised his voice and shouted:
"May Baal rebuild Hirgab's wings,
   may Baal rebuild his pinions;
   Hirgab, up, and fly away!"
When he raised his eyes and looked,
   he saw Samal, the mother of vultures.
He raised his voice and shouted:
"May Baal shatter Samal's wings,
   may Baal shatter her pinions;
   let her fall at my feet.
I will split her gizzard and look;
   if there is fat, if there is bone,
I will weep and I will bury him,
   I will put him into the hole of the gods of the earth."
These words had just come from his mouth,
   this speech from his lips,
when Baal shattered Samal's wings,
   Baal shattered her pinions,
   she fell at his feet.
He split her gizzard and looked:
   there was fat, there was bone.
From them he took Aqhat . . .
he wept and he buried him,
   he buried him in a grave, in an urn.
Then he raised his voice and shouted:
"May Baal shatter the vultures' wings,

       may Baal shatter their pinions,
if they fly over my son's grave
     and wake him from his sleep."
The king cursed Qor-maym:
"Woe to you, Qor-maym,
       for near you Aqhat the Hero was killed,
       the young lion of El's house met his end.
Now flee forever,
       from now on and forevermore."
Then he destroyed his royal scepter.
He arrived at Mararat-tagullal-banir;
       he raised his voice and shouted:
"Woe to you, Mararat-tagullal-banir,
       for near you Aqhat the Hero was killed.
May your root not rise from the ground,
       your head droop because you have been plucked.
Now flee forever,
       from now on and forevermore."
Then he destroyed his royal scepter.
He arrived at the city of Abiluma,
       Abiluma, the city of Prince Moon.
He raised his voice and shouted:
"Woe to you, city of Abiluma,
       for near you Aqhat the Hero was killed.
May Baal make you blind, now and forever,
       from now on and forevermore."
Then he destroyed his royal scepter.
Danel arrived at his house,
       Danel reached his palace.
The keeners entered his palace,
       the mourners his court;
those who gash their skin wept,
       they shed tears for Aqhat the Hero,
       the child of Danel, the Healer's man.
The days became months,
       the months became years;

for seven years they wept for Aqhat the Hero,
>they shed tears for the child of Danel, the Healer's man.
Then, in the seventh year, Danel, the Healer's man, spoke;
>the Hero, the man of the god of Harnam, raised his
>voice and shouted:
"Leave my house, keeners;
>leave my palace, mourners,
>leave my court, you who gash your skin."
He made a sacrifice to the gods,
>he sent an offering up to heaven,
>an offering for the god of Harnam to the stars. . . .
Pagat who got up early to draw water spoke:
"My father, you have made a sacrifice to the gods,
>you have sent an offering up to heaven,
>an offering for the god of Harnam to the stars.
Now bless me, that I may go with your blessing;
>favor me, that I may go with your favor.
I will kill my brother's killer,
>put an end to whoever put an end to my mother's son."
Danel, the Healer's man, replied:
"Pagat, you will restore my life,
you who get up early to draw water,
>who brush the dew from the barley,
>who know the course of the stars;
I will truly live again
when you have killed your brother's killer,
>put an end to whoever put an end to your mother's
>son."
She washed in the sea,
>using a sea dye she put on rouge,
>applied special cosmetics from the sea.
She put on a hero's clothes,
>she placed a knife in her sheath,
>she placed a sword in her scabbard;
and over all this she put on women's clothes.
As Sun, the gods' torch, went in,

Pagat entered the fields;
as Sun, the gods' torch, set,
Pagat arrived at the tents.
Word was brought to Yatpan:
"Our mistress has come to your pavilion,
Pagat has come to the tents."
And Yatpan, the Lady's man, replied:
"Receive her: she'll give me wine to drink;
she'll take the cup from my hand,
the mug from my right hand."
Pagat was received; she gave him a drink;
she took the cup from his hand,
the mug from his right hand.
Then Yatpan, the Lady's man, said:
". . . The hand that killed Aqhat the Hero
can kill a thousand enemies. . . ."
Twice she gave him wine to drink,
she gave him wine to drink.

. . . .

THE HEALERS

INTRODUCTION

The three fragmentary and obscure tablets called *The Healers,* of which parts of two are translated below, are a possible sequel to *Aqhat.* We include them here despite their difficulty because they mention Danel, Aqhat's father, and because they were written down by Ilimilku.

The principal figures in the tablets, after which they are named, are called "Healers" or by some commentators "Hale Ones." Their identification and function are far from clear. Some scholars consider them human beings who performed certain cultic functions; others see them as divine attendants of El. A third school, with which we agree, understands the Healers to be minor deities of the underworld. Most probably they were the deified dead ancestors of the family who looked after the interests of their living relatives, especially with regard to agricultural and human fertility. The existence of a cult of dead ancestors among the Canaanites is suggested by the lines describing the duties of the ideal son in *Aqhat*—he will " 'set up a stele for his divine ancestor, a family shrine in the sanctuary' "; by the divine blessing of Kirta—" 'May Kirta be highly praised, in the midst of the Healers of the earth, in the assembly of the Gatherers of Ditan' "; and by other texts not translated here.

In the context of the story of Aqhat, we can interpret the visit of the Healers to the threshing floor and plantations as intended to heal the crops that had been affected by Aqhat's death. Similarly, the mention of a son and grandson implies the concern of the Healers for the continuation of the family. It may well be that Aqhat, like Baal, was brought back to life by the Healers.

This understanding of the Healers as gods of the underworld is supported by references to beings with the same name in later sources. In the Bible, the Rephaim (the term is a variant of the

Ugaritic *rp'um*, "Healers") comprised two groups. The first are inhabitants of the underworld, often called "shades," and appear in such passages as Job 26:5: "The Rephaim below tremble, the waters and their inhabitants." This is also the connotation of the term in two Phoenician burial inscriptions, which threatened anyone opening the tomb with this curse: "May they have no home with the Healers; may they not be buried in a grave; may they have no son or descendant in their place." (Note the association of offspring with the Healers.)

The other identification of the term in the Bible is as a race of giants who lived in parts of the land of Canaan before the arrival of the Israelites. The Israelites could well have extended the meaning of the word to include not only the deified ancestors of the Canaanites they displaced, but the Canaanites themselves.

Finally, we wish to call attention to the association of Baal with the Healers at the end of this text. As a god who fell under Death's power yet returned to provide for "earth's masses," Baal was prototypical of the Healers. They too bridged the chasm between this world and the next, perhaps with Baal as their divine patron. Just as the forces of sterility and drought that controlled the land during Baal's absence in the underworld were dispelled by the fertility god's revival, so the drought that followed Aqhat's death was ended with the Healers' help when Aqhat (or a substitute) was restored to life and returned to Danel, "the Healer's man."

THE HEALERS

I

. . . .
". . . eight in the midst of my palace."
To his place the Healers went,
  to his place went the divine ones. . . .
They mounted their chariots;
  they went on their asses;
they traveled one day, then a second;
  after sunset on the third,
the Healers arrived at the threshing floor,
  the divine ones at the plantations.
And Danel, the Healer's man, spoke:
"Healers, enter the threshing floor,
  divine ones, come into the plantations. . . ."
. . . .

II

. . . .
"Behold your son,
  behold . . . your grandson . . .
  the small one will kiss your lips . . .
. . . .
When Anat went hunting,
  she shot the birds of heaven.
They slaughtered oxen,
  they killed sheep,
  bulls, fatling rams,
  yearling calves;
they strangled lambs and kids. . . .
One day passed, then two:
  the Healers ate and drank.

Three days passed, then four;
    five days passed, then six:
    the Healers ate and drank.
Then, on the seventh day,
    Baal the Conqueror. . . .

. . . .

KIRTA

INTRODUCTION

Divinity doth hedge a king.
Hamlet, Act IV, Sc. v

The centrality of kingship as a Canaanite institution is well illustrated by the three tablets containing the story of Kirta. The surviving episodes are parts of a larger cycle, in which there was at least one more tablet after those translated here; the final column of the third tablet is fully preserved and ends in the middle of a sentence. Though we have no indication of exactly how much is missing, we can suppose that there were episodes before and after each of the other tablets. Nevertheless, while the narrative as we have it is not the whole story, each episode is largely self-contained and therefore understandable. The Arthurian legends provide a good parallel; in them a theme such as the quest for the Holy Grail loosely ties together various characters and plots.

The hero of the cycle is a king, whose name was pronounced Kirta or perhaps Keret, and the basic theme that unites the episodes is the survival of his dynasty. The first tablet opens with a statement of Kirta's predicament: his once numerous family had perished, and he had no descendants. Kirta's situation recalls that of Job, a comparison strengthened by Kirta's sickness described in the second and third tablets. But whereas Job's problems followed one another quickly, Kirta's were spread out over a long period, and each difficulty forms a separate episode. There are also echoes of *Aqhat;* like Danel when he was childless, Kirta seems to have performed an incubation rite, during which El, his patron and perhaps his father, appeared to him in a dream.

In this dream Kirta was given detailed instructions to offer a sacrifice to the gods and then to prepare for war. The war was to be total—all segments of the population had to serve or provide a substitute—and its purpose was to sue for the hand of the daughter of the king of a city about seven days' march away. The sketches of the mustering of the army and the siege of Pabil's city are reminiscent of Homer's description of the shield of Achilles, on which Hephaistos depicted various scenes from human life, including a city at peace and a city under siege. Kirta's dream went on to foretell his negotiations with Pabil after seven days of siege; in them Kirta demanded Pabil's daughter Hurriya in marriage. Hurriya's beauty is compared to that of Anat and Astarte, and she is described like the statue of a goddess with inlaid eyebrows and jewels for eyes.

With the repetition typical of ancient narrative poetry, the instructions given in the dream are repeated virtually line for line as Kirta carried them out. There is only one significant variant: en route to Pabil's city Udm, Kirta stopped at a shrine of Asherah, where he promised an offering to the goddess if his quest proved successful.

Events turned out as the dream had prophesied, for in the second and least complete of the tablets El blessed Kirta's marriage in the presence of the Assembly of the gods and promised him many children, of which even the youngest would have a large inheritance. Kirta, however, neglected to fulfill his vow to Asherah and was punished by being stricken with an unnamed but debilitating disease, evidently just before a feast to which he had invited the peers of his realm, his "seventy noble bulls, eighty noble gazelles." (The aristocracy of the Canaanites, like their pantheon, often had animal names as titles.)

The third tablet begins with a speech by Ilihu, one of Kirta's sons, urging his father to accept the fact of his imminent death. The king's sickness had had a catastrophic effect: as though in sympathy, nature had failed and famine threatened. It seemed that Kirta had to die, despite the fact that he was in some sense El's son (see below). Nevertheless, moved by the prayers of the people of Hubur, the capital city, or of Kirta's family, or perhaps of the sick king himself, El decided to intervene. The disease was so virulent that none of the other gods dared to try to cure it, so El pledged to act personally. He sent the goddess of healing, Shataqat, who with El's power overcame the disease and dispelled Death. The sickness itself is not described in detail, but it involved a fever that Shataqat was able to break. Kirta regained his appetite and resumed his rule.

His troubles, however, had not ended. Yassib, another of his sons, threatened to oust Kirta from the throne on the grounds that he had not fully recovered and that his illness had caused him to neglect the essential duties of kingship. Kirta responded with a curse on his son, and here the story breaks off.

As this summary of the contents of the three extant tablets of the *Kirta* cycle shows, Kirta had to face three problems as a king: his childlessness, his illness, and his son's challenge. Without an heir or a wife to provide one, the dynasty was doomed to extinction. If a civil war should occur as the result of an uncertain succession, Kirta would have failed in one of his essential duties, the preservation of order; one key function of kingship in the ancient world was the maintenance of stability, so that the subjects of the realm would not be disturbed in their prescribed tasks. This required the promulgation of laws to regulate the relations between citizens, the defeat or deterrence of enemies from the outside, and the guarantee of a smooth transfer of power from the king to his successor. His childlessness prevented Kirta from fulfilling the third of these responsibilities, and this is the motivation for the first episode, which recounts the search for a wife.

The problem of Kirta's illness also affected the social order, for while he was sick there was no one to defend the powerless —widows and orphans, the poor, and the oppressed. His son Yassib attempted, presumably unsuccessfully, to usurp the throne, on the grounds that Kirta was incapable of ruling. This episode, unfortunately incomplete, is similar to Absalom's revolt against his father David as narrated in II Samuel 15. Absalom exploited David's failure to provide justice for his subjects, and won such widespread popular support that his father was forced to flee across the Jordan until the rebellion had been crushed.

The stories of David and Kirta are linked by another parallel. As we have observed, one of the themes that recurs in the *Kirta* cycle is the problem of succession. A similar emphasis has been found in a literary unit in the Bible comprising II Samuel 9–20 and I Kings 1–2, a document that has been styled "the Succession History of David" since the central thread of the narrative is the question of who would succeed David on the throne of Israel. The last episode in the "Succession History" describes the struggle between two of David's sons, Adonijah and Solomon, over the kingship. David was still alive, though advanced in years and evidently senile, and the court as well as the religious and military leaders was divided into factions supporting one claimant or the other. Again a king's lack of health caused the breakdown of the social order.

Kingship in the ancient world, however, was not just a political and social institution; it was also religious, or sacral. Kings were representatives of their people to the gods; Kirta, for example, clearly functioned as a priest in offering sacrifice to El and to Baal, and he was actually present at the divine Assembly when El and the other gods blessed his marriage. In addition, and perhaps because he was a member of the divine Assembly, the king was responsible for the prosperity of his subjects. There was a direct connection between the health of the king and the agricultural cycle, or, more accurately, the king and the gods were jointly responsible for the harvest. When Baal died, Death reigned and nothing grew; when the king was ill, the crops failed and famine resulted. Thus Kirta's sickness, the subject of the cycle's second episode, was a failure of kingship, but because of his quasidivine status the gods were also implicated in its consequences.

The king was a man, and yet was the head of human society; the gods communicated with him, yet he was not fully a god. This ambiguity may be clarified by an examination of Kirta's titles. He is called "the Lad of El," "El's servant," and "El's son." The first two epithets are synonymous and express Kirta's close, although subordinate, relationship with El. It is possible that the third title is to be taken literally, and that Kirta, who many have suggested was the legendary founder of the royal house of Ugarit, may have been El's son by a human mother; there are parallels to divine parentage of the founders of cities and dynasties in Greco-Roman mythology. But the Canaanite ideology of kingship has closer reflections in the Bible; the Israelites borrowed the institution of the monarchy and much of its concomitant ritual and idiom from their neighbors. We are therefore justified in subsuming Ugaritic and biblical evidence under one heading, and in using each to interpret the other.

The biblical sources are especially helpful in interpreting Kirta's designation as "El's son." In the coronation hymn that appears in the Bible as Psalm 2, the king speaks:

I will tell of Yahweh's decree;
he said to me: "You are my son;
   this day I have begotten you."

The same proclamation is put into the mouths of the divine Assembly in Isaiah 9:6:

For unto us a child has been born,
   unto us a son has been given.

Other uses of the father-son image to describe the king's relationship to the gods are found in II Samuel 7:14 and Psalm 89:26; taken together with the Ugaritic evidence they suggest that the coronation ritual included the adoption of the newly crowned king as son of the national god. It is best, therefore, not to understand Kirta's title in a biological sense.

Despite his status as El's adopted son, Kirta was still a mortal; he had to die, and he should not yearn

"to rule like the Bull, his father,
   or to have power like the Father of Men."

For the Canaanites, unlike the Egyptians with whom they had commercial contacts and by whom they were influenced, did not believe that the king was a god; to be son of god was to remain human.

KIRTA

Ruined was the house of the king
    who once had seven brothers,
    eight sons of one mother.
Kirta our patriarch was destroyed,
    Kirta's dynasty was finished.
His legal wife went away,
    his lawful spouse:
    the woman he married left him.
He had had descendants,
    but one third died in childbirth,
    one fourth of disease,
    one fifth Resheph gathered to himself,
    one sixth were lost at sea,
    one seventh fell in battle.
Kirta saw his offspring,
    he saw his offspring destroyed,
    his royal house completely finished.
His line was utterly ruined,
    and he had no heir in his household.
He entered his room and wept,
    he repeated his words and shed tears;
his tears poured
    like shekels to the ground,
    like fifth-shekels onto his bed.
As he wept he fell asleep,
    as he shed tears he had a dream;
sleep overpowered him and he lay down,
    but his dream made him restless.
For in his dream El came down,
    in his vision the Father of Men.

He approached and asked Kirta:
"Why are you weeping, Kirta?
    why does the Gracious One, the Lad of El, shed tears?
Does he want to rule like the Bull, his father,
    or to have power like the Father of Men?"
. . . .
"Why should I want silver and gleaming gold,
    a controlling share in a mine,
perpetual slaves, three horses,
    a chariot from the stable, servants?
Let me have sons,
    let me produce descendants!"
And the Bull, his father El, replied:
"No more weeping, Kirta,
    nor tears, Gracious One, Lad of El.
Wash yourself and put on rouge,
    wash your arm to the elbow,
    from your fingers to your shoulder.
Enter the shade of your tent,
take a lamb in your hand,
    a sacrificial lamb in your right hand,
    a young animal in both your hands,
all the food which accompanies the libation.
Take the proper sacrificial bird,
pour wine from a silver goblet,
    honey from a golden bowl,
and go up to the top of the tower,
    climb to the height of the wall;
raise your hands to heaven,
    sacrifice to the Bull, your father El;
serve Baal with your sacrifice,
    the son of Dagon with your provisions.
Then let Kirta come down from the roof,
let him prepare food for the city,
    grain for Bit-Hubur;
let him bake enough bread for five months,

enough food for six.
Let the populace be supplied and come out,
    let the special forces be supplied
    and the populace come out.
Your army will be powerful indeed,
    three hundred thousand strong,
serfs beyond counting,
    archers beyond reckoning.
The infantry will advance in thousands,
    and in ten thousands, like the early rain;
they will advance two by two,
    three by three, all together.
The bachelor will close his house;
    the widow will hire a substitute;
the sick man will carry his bed;
    the blind man will be assigned a station;
even the new husband will come out:
    he will entrust his wife to another,
    his love to a stranger.
Like the locusts which live in the fields,
    like grasshoppers at the edge of the desert,
advance one day, and a second,
    three days, then four,
    five days, then six.
Then, at sunset on the seventh day,
you will arrive at Udm the great,
    Udm the well-watered;
and attack the cities,
    raid the towns;
drive the woodcutters from the fields,
    the gatherers of straw from the threshing floors;
drive the water carriers from the well,
    the women filling their jars from the spring.
Wait one day, and a second,
    three days, then four,
    five days, then six.

Don't shoot your arrows at the city,
     your slingstones at the fortress.
Then, by sunset on the seventh day,
     King Pabil will be unable to sleep
because of the sound of his horses neighing,
     because of the noise of his asses braying,
because of the lowing of his plow oxen,
     because of the howl of his sheepdog.
And he will send messengers to you,
     to Kirta his peer:
'Message of King Pabil:
Take silver and gleaming gold,
     a controlling share in a mine,
perpetual slaves, three horses,
     a chariot from the stable, servants;
Kirta, take these as peace offerings,
     and leave my house, king,
     go away from my court, Kirta.
Do not lay siege to Udm the great,
     Udm the well-watered:
for Udm is El's gift,
     and a present from the Father of Men.'
Then you will send messengers back to him:
'Why should I want silver and gleaming gold,
     a controlling share in a mine,
perpetual slaves, three horses,
     a chariot from the stable, servants?
Give me rather what is not in my house:
     give me the Lady Hurriya,
     the fairest of your first-born:
her fairness is like Anat's,
     her beauty is like Astarte's,
her eyebrows are lapis lazuli,
     her eyes are jeweled bowls. . . .
I will rest in the gaze of her eyes.
This in my dream El granted,

in my vision the Father of Men;
she will bear offspring for Kirta,
    a boy for El's servant.' "
Kirta looked, and it was a dream:
    El's servant had had a vision.
He washed himself and put on rouge,
    he washed his arm to the elbow,
    from his fingers to his shoulder.
He entered the shade of the tent,
he took a lamb in his hand,
    a sacrificial lamb in his right hand,
    a young animal in both his hands,
all the food which accompanies the libation.
He took the proper sacrificial bird,
he poured wine from a silver goblet,
    honey from a golden bowl,
and he went up to the top of the tower,
    he climbed to the height of the wall;
he raised his hands to heaven,
    he sacrificed to the Bull, his father El;
he served Baal with his sacrifice,
    the son of Dagon with his provisions.
Kirta came down from the roof,
he prepared food for the city,
    grain for Bit-Hubur;
he baked enough bread for five months,
    enough food for six.
The populace was supplied and came out,
    the special forces were supplied
    and the populace came out.
His army was powerful indeed,
    three hundred thousand strong.
The infantry advanced in thousands,
    and in ten thousands, like the early rain;
they advanced two by two,
    three by three, all together.

The bachelor closed his house;
    the widow hired a substitute,
the sick man carried his bed,
    the blind man was assigned a station;
even the new husband came out:
    he entrusted his wife to another,
    his love to a stranger.
Like the locusts which live in the fields,
    like grasshoppers at the edge of the desert,
they advanced one day, and a second;
    then, at sunset on the third day,
they arrived at the shrine of Asherah of Tyre,
    and of the goddess of Sidon.
There Kirta the Noble made a vow:
"As Asherah of Tyre lives,
    and the goddess of Sidon,
if I take Hurriya to my house,
    if I bring the maiden to my court,
then I will give double her price in silver,
    and triple her price in gold."
They advanced one day, and a second,
    three days, then four;
after sunset on the fourth day
they arrived at Udm the great,
    Udm the well-watered.
They attacked the cities,
    they raided the towns;
they drove the woodcutters from the fields,
    and the gatherers of straw from the threshing floors;
they drove the water carriers from the well,
    and the women filling their jars from the spring.
He waited one day, then a second,
    three days, then four,
    five days, then six;
then, by sunset on the seventh day,
    King Pabil was unable to sleep

because of the sound of his horses neighing,
    because of the noise of his asses braying,
because of the lowing of his plow oxen,
    because of the howl of his sheepdog.
Then King Pabil called to his wife . . . .

. . . .

"Then head toward Kirta, my peer,
    and say to Kirta the Noble:
'Message of King Pabil:
Take silver and gleaming gold,
    a controlling share in a mine,
perpetual slaves, three horses,
    a chariot from the stable, servants;
Kirta, take these as peace offerings;
do not lay siege to Udm the great,
    Udm the well-watered:
for Udm is El's gift,
    and a present from the Father of Men.
Go away from my house, king,
    leave my court, Kirta.' ". . .
The two messengers left; they did not turn back;
    they headed toward Kirta, his peer;
they raised their voices and shouted:
"Message of King Pabil:
Take silver and gleaming gold,
    a controlling share in a mine,
and perpetual slaves, three horses,
    a chariot from the stable, servants;
Kirta, take these as peace offerings;
do not lay siege to Udm the great,
    Udm the well-watered:
for Udm is El's gift,
    a present from the Father of Men.
Go away from my house, king,
    leave my court, Kirta."
And Kirta the Noble replied:

"Why should I want silver and gleaming gold,
    a controlling share in a mine,
and perpetual slaves, three horses,
    a chariot from the stable, servants?
Give me rather what is not in my house:
    give me the Lady Hurriya,
    the fairest of your first-born:
her fairness is like Anat's,
    her beauty is like Astarte's,
her eyebrows are lapis lazuli,
    her eyes are jeweled bowls.
This in my dream El granted,
    in my vision the Father of Men;
she will bear offspring for Kirta,
    a boy for El's servant."
The two messengers left; they did not turn back;
    they headed toward King Pabil;
they raised their voices and shouted:
"Message of Kirta the Noble,
    the word of the Gracious One, the Lad of El."

II

. . . .
"She leads the hungry by the hand,
    she leads the thirsty by the hand . . .
    to Kirta, his peer.
As the cow lows for her calf,
    as recruits long for their mothers,
    so Udm will sigh."
And Kirta the Noble answered . . .

. . . .
    . . . the Bull,
    . . . Baal the Conqueror,
    . . . Prince Moon,

... Kothar-wa-Hasis,
... the Maiden, Prince Resheph,
and the Assembly of the gods in procession. ...
The Assembly of the gods arrived,
    and Baal the Conqueror said:
"Come now, El the Kind, the Compassionate:
bless Kirta the Noble,
    show your favor to the Gracious One, the Lad of El."
El took a cup in his hand,
    a goblet in his right hand;
he pronounced a blessing over his servant,
    El blessed Kirta the Noble,
    he showed his favor to the Gracious One, the Lad of El:
"Kirta, you have taken a wife,
    you have taken a wife into your house,
    you have brought a maiden into your court.
She will bear you seven sons,
    she will produce eight for you;
she will bear Yassib the Lad,
    who will drink the milk of Asherah,
    suck the breasts of the Virgin Anat,
    the two wet nurses of the gods."
. . . .
"May Kirta be highly praised,
    in the midst of the Healers of the earth,
    in the assembly of the Gatherers of Ditan.
She will soon bear you daughters:
    she will bear the girl . . .
    she will bear the girl . . .
    she will bear the girl . . .
    she will bear the girl . . .
    she will bear the girl . . .
    she will bear the girl . . . .
May Kirta be highly praised,
    in the midst of the Healers of the earth,
    in the assembly of the Gatherers of Ditan;

to the youngest I will give a first-born's rights."
The gods pronounced their blessing and went,
    the gods went to their tents,
    the Council of El to their divine homes.
And she soon bore him sons,
    and she soon bore him daughters.
Then, after seven years,
the sons of Kirta were as many as had been promised;
    so too were the daughters of Hurriya.
And Asherah remembered his vow,
    the goddess recalled his pledge;
and she raised her voice and shouted:
"Look now, has Kirta changed his vow?
    I will break . . . ."
. . . .
He called to his wife:
"Listen, Lady Hurriya:
slaughter your fattest animal;
    open a jar of wine;
call my seventy noble bulls,
    my eighty noble gazelles,
the noble bulls of Hubur the great,
    of Hubur the well-watered. . . ."
Lady Hurriya obeyed;
she slaughtered her fattest animal;
    she opened a jar of wine;
she invited the noble bulls into her presence,
    she invited the noble gazelles into her presence,
the noble bulls of Hubur the great,
    of Hubur the well-watered.
They came to Kirta's house,
    to his home . . . .
She extended her hand to the bowl,
    she put her knife to the meat,
and the Lady Hurriya said:
"I have called you to eat and drink

at the banquet of Kirta your master."
. . . .
She extended her hand to the bowl,
    she put her knife to the meat,
and the Lady Hurriya said:
"I have called you to eat and drink . . . ."
They wept for Kirta,
    the noble bulls spoke,
        they wept as though he were dead. . . .
"At sunset Kirta will surely arrive,
    at sundown our master will rule. . . ."
. . . .
And the Lady Hurriya said:
"I have called you to eat and drink
    at the banquet of Kirta your lord."
They came to Kirta,
    their words were like the words of noble bulls.
In a vision . . . Kirta . . .
. . . .

III

"As a dog is removed from your house,
    a hound from your court,
so you too, father, must die like a mortal,
    and your court become a place of mourning,
        controlled by women, beloved father.
Baal's mountain, father, will weep for you,
    Zaphon, the holy stronghold,
the holy stronghold will lament,
    the stronghold wide and broad:
'Is not Kirta El's son,
    an offspring of the Kind and Holy One?' "
He entered his father's presence;
    he wept and gnashed his teeth;
    he spoke through his tears:

"Our father, we were glad while you seemed to live forever,
    we rejoiced at your immortality;
but as a dog is removed from your house,
    a hound from your court,
so you too, father, must die like a mortal,
    and your court become a place of mourning,
    controlled by women, beloved father.
How can it be said that Kirta is El's son,
    an offspring of the Kind and Holy One?
Or do the gods die?
    Will the Kind One's offspring not live on?"
But Kirta the Noble replied:
"My son, don't weep,
    don't grieve for me;
my son, don't drain the well of your eyes,
    your head's springs of tears.
Call your sister Thitmanit,
    a maiden whose ardor is strong:
she will weep and grieve for me . . . .
Speak to your sister . . .
    I know how loving she is:
she will make her cry heard in the fields,
    her spirit's outpourings in the sky.
. . . the setting of Lady Sun,
    and the light of the Ten Thousand shines.
Then say to your sister Thitmanit:
'Our Kirta has prepared a banquet,
    the king has ordered a feast.
Take your drum in your hand,
    your lyre in your right hand;
go stand by your lord's singers . . . .' "
Then the Hero Ilihu
    took his spear in his hand,
    his lance in his right hand,
and he approached at a run.
As he arrived, it grew dark;

his sister was coming out to draw water.
He put his spear on the hill,
    he went to meet her at the gate.
As soon as she saw her brother,
    her back was as though shattered on the ground;
    when she saw her brother, she wept.
"Is the king sick?
    Is Kirta your lord ill?"
And the Hero Ilihu replied:
"The king is not sick;
    Kirta your lord is not ill.
But he has prepared a banquet,
    the king has ordered a feast. . . ."
. . . .
She approached her brother and shouted:
"Why did you deceive me, my brother?
How many months has he been sick?
    how long has he been ill?"
And the Hero Ilihu replied:
"He has been sick for three months,
    Kirta has been ill for four.
His end is at hand:
        prepare a grave,
        prepare a grave,
        make ready a tomb." . . .
She prepared a grave . . .
she wept and gnashed her teeth;
    she spoke through her tears:
"Our father, we were glad while you seemed to live forever,
    we rejoiced at your immortality;
but as a dog is removed from your house,
    a hound from your court,
so you too, father, must die like a mortal,
    and your court become a place of mourning,
    controlled by women, beloved father.
Or do the gods die?

Will the Kind One's offspring not live on?
Baal's mountain, father, will weep for you,
    Zaphon, the holy stronghold,
the holy stronghold will lament,
    the stronghold wide and broad:
'Is not Kirta El's son,
    an offspring of the Kind and Holy One?' "
. . . .
. . . Baal's rain for the earth,
    and the rain of the Most High for the fields;
for Baal's rain benefits the earth,
    and the rain of the Most High the fields,
benefits the wheat in the furrow,
    the spelt in the tilled ground. . . .
The plowmen lifted their heads,
    the sowers of grain their backs:
gone was the food from their bins,
    gone was the wine from their skins,
    gone was the oil from their vats.
. . . .
"El has heard your speech:
look—you are wise, like El,
    like the Bull, the Kind One;
call to Ilisha, the carpenter god,
    Ilisha, the carpenter of Baal's house,
    and his wives, the carpenter goddesses. . . ."
He called to Ilisha, the carpenter god,
    Ilisha, the carpenter of Baal's house,
    and his wives, the carpenter goddesses.
And El the Kind, the Compassionate, replied:
"Listen, Ilisha, carpenter god,
    Ilisha, the carpenter of Baal's house,
    and your wives, the carpenter goddesses:
go up to the height of the building . . . ."
. . . .
And El the Kind, the Compassionate, replied:

"Who among the gods can expel the sickness,
      drive out the disease?"
But none of the gods answered him.
He spoke a second, then a third time:
"Who among the gods can expel the sickness,
      drive out the disease?"
But none of the gods answered him.
He spoke a fourth, then a fifth time:
"Who among the gods can expel the sickness,
      drive out the disease?"
But none of the gods answered him.
He spoke a sixth, then a seventh time:
"Who among the gods can expel the sickness,
      drive out the disease?"
But none of the gods answered him.
Then El the Kind, the Compassionate, replied:
"My sons, sit down upon your thrones,
      upon your princely seats.
I will work magic,
      I will bring relief:
I will expel the sickness,
      I will drive out the disease."
. . . .
"Death—be broken!
      Shataqat—be strong!"
And Shataqat left;
      she came to Kirta's house:
in tears she entered and went in,
      in sobs she went inside.
She flew over cities . . .
      she flew over villages . . .
      . . . the sickness on its head.
She returned, she washed off his sweat;
      she restored his appetite for food,
      his desire for a meal.
Death was broken—

Shataqat was strong!
Then Kirta the Noble gave a command;
    he raised his voice and shouted:
"Listen, Lady Hurriya:
slaughter a lamb so that I may eat,
    some mutton for my meal."
Lady Hurriya obeyed:
she slaughtered a lamb and he ate,
    some mutton for his meal.
One day had ended, and on the second
Kirta sat on his throne,
    he sat on his royal chair,
    on his dais, on the seat of dominion.
Now Yassib too lived in the palace,
    and his heart instructed him:
"Go to your father, Yassib,
    go to your father and speak,
    repeat to Kirta your lord:
'Listen closely and pay attention:
as though raiders had raided, you will be driven out,
    and forced to live in the mountains.
Weakness has stayed your hand:
you do not judge the cases of widows,
    you do not preside over the hearings of the oppressed;
the sickbed has become your brother,
    the stretcher your close friend.
Come down from the kingship—let me be king,
    from your power—let me sit on the throne.' "
Yassib the Lad left;
    he entered his father's presence;
    he raised his voice and shouted:
"Listen, Kirta the Noble,
    listen closely and pay attention:
as though raiders had raided, you will be driven out,
    and forced to live in the mountains.
Weakness has stayed your hand:

you do not judge the cases of widows,
you do not preside over the hearings of the oppressed;
you do not drive out those who plunder the poor,
you do not feed the orphan before you,
the widow behind your back.
The sickbed has become your brother,
the stretcher your close friend.
Come down from the kingship—let me be king,
from your power—let me sit on the throne."
But Kirta the Noble replied:
"My son, may Horon smash,
may Horon smash your head,
Astarte, Baal's other self, your skull.
May you fall at the prime of your life . . . ."

The scribe was Ilimilku the Noble.

BAAL

INTRODUCTION

" 'Our king is Baal the Conqueror.' " This affirmation is the theme of the *Baal* cycle. *Kirta* describes the role of the human king of a Canaanite city-state; the six tablets that contain Attanu-Purlianni and Ilimilku's version of *Baal* narrate the story of Baal's rise to kingship over the gods by his defeat of the forces of chaos, Sea and Death. The struggles through which Baal proved himself and the challenges he met reflect the process by which Baal became the most important deity in Ugaritic theology. Apart from the texts translated here, eight other tablets, all in bad condition, contain variants and other episodes of the cycle, attesting to its importance and to the preeminence of its divine hero in Ugarit.

The first episode begins with Sea's demand that the Assembly of the gods surrender Baal to him. The Council was terrified by the rude menacing approach of Sea's envoys, and despite Baal's willingness to act as the gods' spokesman, it was El, the head of the Assembly, who replied to the messengers and promised to hand Baal over to Sea.

Baal's ambitions are evident: he would be the leader of the gods; his rebuke of them underlines his courage. But who was Sea, and why did the gods fear him? For an answer we must leave Ugarit and move to Mesopotamia, where the Babylonian epic *Enuma Elish* provides some illuminating parallels.

Enuma Elish, named after its opening words "When on high," is a long poem describing the assumption of supreme power among the gods by Marduk, the national god of Babylon. The epic begins with a theogony, relating the origin of the pantheon from the mingling of the waters of Tiamat, the sea, and Apsu, the sweet water. The younger generations of gods were noisy and rambunctious, and Apsu complained:

"By day I find no relief, nor repose by night.
I will destroy, I will wreck their ways,
That quiet may be restored. Let us have rest!"

His plans, however, were discovered, and he was killed by the other gods. This enraged Tiamat, and although she had earlier been unwilling to see her children put to death, now "she prepared for battle against the gods, her offspring." The gods were alarmed:

"No god" (thought they) "can go to battle and,
Facing Tiamat, escape with his life."

The only deity strong enough to resist was Marduk, and he became the champion of the gods, receiving absolute authority in heaven and on earth.

The fuller account in the Babylonian poem provides the motivation for the gods' fear missing in the Ugaritic text. But there are differences. Tiamat, whose name means "sea," was female, while the Canaanite Prince Sea was male. Tiamat was the mother of the first generation of gods, and thus the ancestor of them all; Prince Sea's genealogy is not known. Finally, in contrast to the antagonism between Tiamat and Anu, the Mesopotamian sky god and El's counterpart, the relationship between Prince Sea and El is harmonious, as evinced by one of Sea's epithets, "El's Darling"; since this same title is applied to Baal's other adversary, Death, and since it was El who promised to surrender Baal to Prince Sea, it may be that El and Sea were at least tacitly allied in wishing to dispose of the young god who was the latter's rival and who challenged the former's position as king.

Despite El's promise, Baal did not submit to Sea, but (aided by two clubs fashioned by Kothar-wa-Hasis) fought with and defeated him. Afterward Astarte proclaimed:

"Hail, Baal the Conqueror!
hail, Rider on the Clouds!
For Prince Sea is our captive,
Judge River is our captive."

While the description of the battle between Baal and Sea is much more terse than that of the contest between Marduk and Tiamat, the characteristics of Baal and Marduk are similar. Both are associated with the storm: Marduk's name probably means "son of the storm," and Baal's title "Rider on the Clouds" recalls Marduk's "storm chariot." Before his contest Marduk had been proclaimed king of the gods, and during the feast that celebrated his victory his praises were sung by the divine Assembly. While Astarte's proclamation, which we have just quoted, is not a declaration of Baal's kingship, it points toward that conclusion, as, in light of the Mesopotamian parallel, does the victory banquet at which Baal's praises were sung.

In the Introduction we have seen that the language used of Baal as storm god is echoed in the description of Yahweh, the god of Israel, who

> makes the clouds his chariot,
> walks on the wings of the wind,
> makes the winds his messengers,
> fire (and) flame his ministers.
> (Psalm 104:3–4)

As Baal defeated Sea, so also did Yahweh:

> With his power he stilled the sea,
> with his skill he smote Rahab,
> with his wind he bagged Sea,
> his hand pierced the fleeing serpent.
> (Job 26:12–13)

Similar mythological language occurs in Psalm 89:9–10 and Isaiah 27:1.

Baal's adversary has the double title "Prince Sea" and "Judge River"; "sea" and "river" occur frequently in biblical poetry as parallel terms. Most interesting in this context is the application of this pair to the two bodies of water that Yahweh mastered, enabling his people to escape Egypt and enter Canaan:

> When Israel came out of Egypt,
> the house of Jacob from people of a

different language . . . .
The sea saw and fled,
the Jordan turned back.
(Psalm 114:1, 3)

Just as the Reed Sea was split so that the Israelites crossed on dry land, so too the Jordan miraculously stopped and the chosen people entered the promised land with dry feet (Exodus 14:22; Joshua 3:13). The repetition of the event is rooted in the old poetic formula: sea and river are two aspects of the same reality.

The *Baal* cycle continues with an interlude in which Anat, Baal's sister and spouse, showed her own prowess in battle. Because the top and bottom of the tablet have broken off, the relationship between this bloody scene with its fanciful sequel and the preceding and following episodes is not clear. It has been suggested that Anat's "battling in the valley" and her "fighting between the two cities" were part of Baal's engagement with Sea; Anat claims credit for the defeat of Baal's enemies in the following section. In any event, Baal sent messengers to Anat to announce his victory, urging her to cease fighting and to visit him.

This visit introduces the second, and longest, of the three episodes of the cycle, the one that recounts the construction of Baal's house. The term "house" must be understood on three levels. It refers in the first place simply to a home, a dwelling. But since Baal was a god, his house was also a temple. Most importantly, although he had demonstrated his supremacy by defeating Sea, Baal could not be considered a king unless he had a royal palace; this is the reason for El's rejection of Baal's claim to kingship:

"Baal has no house like the other gods',
no court like Asherah's sons'."

Apparently at Anat's insistence, El gave his permission for the construction of a house by Kothar-wa-Hasis for Baal; but El's wife Asherah, whose sons had royal ambitions themselves, also had to give her consent. The relations between Baal and Anat on one side and Asherah on the other were cool at best, and when Baal, bearing gifts, visited Asherah to ask for her approval of his building project, his reception was not to his taste. Despite his outburst, however, Asherah was won over by the bribe, and she joined Anat in promoting the construction of a house for Baal. She furthermore prophesied that when the building was complete, Baal's powers as god of the storm would be manifest:

> "Baal will begin the rainy season,
>   the season of wadis in flood;
> and he will sound his voice in the clouds,
>   flash his lightning to the earth."

Permission having been granted, Kothar visited Baal to receive his instructions, and then the house was built, using the finest cedar in the Lebanon as well as gold, silver, and lapis lazuli. In a reverse alchemy, the precious construction materials turned into blocks and bricks after seven days of firing. Baal celebrated the erection of his palace by inviting the gods to a lavish banquet.

Alert readers may be puzzled by the illogicality of these lines:

> " 'Call a caravan into your house,
>   a wagon train inside your palace . . . .
> And build a house of silver and gold,
>   a house of purest lapis lazuli.' "

Since the theme of this episode is the construction of a house for Baal, it is strange to bid him summon building materials to his house. This seems to be an example of the mechanical use of a formula consisting of the first two lines, and the inconsistency its use caused apparently did not trouble the Canaanites.

The construction of a house for the victorious storm god is also the sequel to Marduk's defeat of Tiamat in *Enuma Elish*. All the gods labored for one year to build Marduk's temple Esagila in the heart of Babylon; when their work was over they sat down to a feast provided by their new king. The possession of a palace was thus a proof of royal status, and this is the reason for the emphasis placed on it in *Baal*. Before his defeat by Baal, Sea had also had a house built for him by Kothar; this is related in the first tablet of the cycle, not translated here because of its mutilated condition.

The Canaanite temples on which the description of Baal's house is based were the primary analogues for the temple of Yahweh in Jerusalem, planned by David and built by his son Solomon. Solomon's architects and craftsmen were Phoenicians who used cedar from the Lebanon for both the temple and the adjacent royal residence. The juxtaposition of temple and palace was deliberate: the deity guaranteed the dynasty and was purposely identified with it. This adoption of Canaanite theory and practice in the house of the god of Israel was responsible for prophetic opposition to the temple from before its construction and until the last days of its existence:

"Thus says Yahweh: Would you build me a house to live in? I have not lived in a house since the day I brought the Israelites up from Egypt until today, but I walked among them with a tent as my divine home. In all the places I walked with the Israelites, did I ever say to one of Israel's judges, whom I commanded to shepherd my people Israel, 'Why haven't you built me a house of cedar?' " (II Samuel 7:5–7)

Despite this conservative resistance the temple was built, and at its dedication Solomon prayed to Yahweh using words that could have been addressed to Baal:

"Give rain to your land, which you gave to your people as their inheritance." (I Kings 8:36)

The acquisition of a house marks the climax of Baal's ascent to the kingship, a climax marked by his theophany in the storm and his assertion,

> "No other king or non-king
> shall set his power over the earth."

Baal's centrality in Ugaritic religion is demonstrable. For instance, a significant index of popular beliefs is the use of divine

elements in personal names; at Ugarit the most frequently occurring deity in names is Baal, including his other names and
titles, such as Hadad.

The transfer of power from an older sky god to a younger
storm god is attested in many contemporary eastern Mediterranean cultures. Kronos was imprisoned and succeeded by his son
Zeus, Yahweh succeeded El as the god of Israel, the Hittite god
Teshub assumed kingship in heaven after having defeated his
father Kumarbi, and Baal replaced El as the effective head of
the Ugaritic pantheon. A more remote and hence less exact
parallel is the replacement of Dyaus by Indra in early Hinduism.
These similar developments can be accurately dated to the second half of the second millennium B.C., a time of prosperity and
extraordinary artistic development, but also of political
upheaval and natural disasters that ended in the collapse or
destruction of many civilizations, including the Mycenaean, Mi-
noan, Hittite, and Ugaritic. This was the period of the Trojan
War, of the invasion of Egypt and the Palestinian coast by the
Sea Peoples, of the international unrest related in the Amarna
letters. In such a context a society might suppose that its traditional objects of worship had proved ineffective, that the pantheon in its established form had, like an entrenched royalty,
become incapable of dealing with new challenges. At this point
it might choose an extradynastic god, as Ugarit chose Baal, son
of Dagon and not of El; and, beset by invasions from the sea and
tidal waves arising from earthquakes, it might construct a mythology in which the new god demonstrated his mastery over
the sea.

This speculative historical reconstruction is weakened by the
possibility that the story of Marduk's defeat of Tiamat, almost
certainly of Mediterranean origin, may date back to the eigh-
teenth century B.C.; we note, however, that the earliest certain
literary evidence for the Babylonian myth does not predate the
first millennium B.C.

We have omitted one aspect of the second episode of *Baal*
because it serves as a transition to the third and final episode;
this is the question of whether Baal's house should have a win-

dow. At first, despite Kothar-wa-Hasis' insistence, Baal refused
to allow the installation of a window, but after the inaugural
banquet and a successful military campaign (only briefly
related), Baal changed his mind, and Kothar "opened a window
in the house." Immediately thereafter Baal revealed himself as
the storm god, declared his sovereignty, and specifically refused
to pay the tribute that was apparently Death's due. The relationship between the window in Baal's house and Death is clarified
by a verse in the book of Jeremiah, one of the rare references
to Death by name in the Bible:

> Death has come up through our windows,
>   he has entered our fortresses,
> cutting down the children in the street
>   and the young men in the squares.
>   (Jeremiah 9:21)

This passage implies a popular superstition that Death entered
a house through a window, and explains Baal's initial reluctance
to include a window in his new house. Though recognized as
king, Baal was unsure of his absolute power, and preferred not
to give Death an opportunity to enter. As we shall see, this
caution was justified. After his theophany Baal became bolder
and rasher, and sent his messengers to inform Death of the
erection of his palace and presumably (though the text is broken
here) of his refusal to pay tribute.

Thus the final episode of *Baal* begins, and it continues with
Death's reply to Baal's delegation. Baal's defeat of Sea, here
called Lotan and the Serpent, had caused a cosmic collapse;
Baal's punishment was that he had to go down into the throat
of Death, whose insatiable appetite is vividly described. The
sequence of the narrative for the remainder of the cycle is difficult to follow, since less than 40 percent of the text is preserved
and translatable. What remains is a series of scenes whose connections are often not clear.

Baal was intimidated by his messengers' report and surren-
dered to Death. After he had had sexual intercourse with "a

heifer," perhaps Anat herself, he descended into the underworld accompanied by his sons and daughters and bringing with him the components of the storm—clouds, wind, lightning bolts, and rain. When news of Baal's death reached El, he began to mourn in typical Semitic fashion. Anat's response was the same, and together with Sun she buried her brother and offered a funerary sacrifice. El's words, repeated by Anat, are an indication of Baal's importance:

> "Baal is dead: what will happen to the peoples?
> Dagon's son: what will happen to the masses?"

The void resulting from Baal's death had to be filled; but neither of the two sons of Asherah who attempted to replace him succeeded in doing so.

The next scene describes two encounters between Anat and Death. In the first Death told how he devoured Baal, and the consequences of this action are intimated: "the heavens shimmered under the sway of El's son Death." With the descent of the storm god into the underworld, the fatal forces of drought and sterility controlled the land; just as the health and prosperity of a city-state depended on the vitality of its ruler, so the survival of the earth and of those who inhabited it was bound up with the existence of "the Lord of the Earth." It was Anat who found the remedy:

> She seized El's son Death:
>> with a sword she split him;
>> with a sieve she winnowed him;
>> with fire she burned him;
>> with a hand mill she ground him;
>> in the fields she sowed him.

Death suffered the various processes that grain has to undergo to make it edible and reproductive. The process by which seed is transformed into a new plant was a mystery to the ancients (as it is to most of us), but it was obviously due to tremendous force:

Unless a grain of wheat falls into the earth and dies, it remains alone; but if it dies, it bears much fruit. (John 12:24)

The death of Death led to Baal's revival; this too was a mystery, but nonetheless a fact: droughts ended, the rains came—Death died, Baal lived. What better way to express this mystery than to describe it in terms of a related phenomenon?

Anat's actions were effective: El had a prophetic dream in which a fabulous fertility was restored to nature; this was a sure sign of Baal's revival. At El's request Sun, the all-seeing eye of heaven, began the search for Baal the Conqueror. "Where is the Prince?"—this cry must have been part of Canaanite ritual, for it recurs as the name of Baal's fanatical devotee Jezebel, the Tyrian princess who became queen of Israel.

Having returned to life, Baal reasserted his power and reclaimed his throne. Then, after seven years, Death challenged him again. The *Baal* cycle ends as it began, with a single combat. As neither of the fighters seemed to be winning, Sun intervened on Baal's behalf, and frightened off Death with her threats. This repetition of the contest between Baal and Death shows that the defeat of the forces of sterility was not permanent. Drought could return, unpredictably and fiercely, once again destroying the fertility that Baal personified. The mention of the seven-year interval makes it clear that the struggle between Death and Baal was not annual, as were analogous struggles in the Greco-Roman world. The Syro-Palestinian climate is in fact not characterized by alternating semiannual cycles of productivity and barrenness. Different crops grow in different seasons, and while the summer is rainless it is not unproductive. But the failure of the winter rains is an agricultural disaster; it is this constant menace that the repetition of the struggle between Baal and Death reflects, that Danel's curse after Aqhat's death promised:

> "For seven years let Baal fail,
>   eight the Rider on the Clouds:
> no dew, no showers,

> no surging of the two seas,
> no benefit of Baal's voice,"

and that David's lament over Saul and Jonathan echoed:

> "Mountains of Gilboa,
>> let there be no rain and no dew upon you,
>> and no showers on the highlands."
>>> (II Samuel 1:21)

Although Sun had an important place in the cult at Ugarit, as witnessed by the lists of offerings, she has a major literary role only in *Baal,* where she helped Anat look for the dead Baal, searched for and found the revivified god, and intervened in his second contest with Death. The abrupt and puzzling ending to Ilimilku and Attanu-Purlianni's version of *Baal* (or at least to as much of the cycle as has been preserved) may be part of a hymn to Lady Sun, "the gods' torch."

BAAL

· ·

I

Sea sent two messengers . . .
"Leave, lads, do not turn back;
now head toward the Assembly in council,
    at the center of the mountain of night.
Do not fall at El's feet,
    do not prostrate yourselves before the Assembly in
        council;
still standing speak your speech,
    repeat your message;
and address the Bull, my father El,
    repeat to the Assembly in council:
'Message of Sea, your master,
    your lord, Judge River:
El, give up the one you are hiding,
    the one the masses are hiding;
give up Baal and his powers,
    the son of Dagon: I will assume his inheritance.' "
The lads left; they did not turn back;
they headed toward the center of the mountain of night,
    the Assembly in council.
There the gods had sat down to eat,
    the holy ones to a meal;
    Baal was standing by El.
As soon as the gods saw them,
    saw the messengers of Sea,
    the mission of Judge River,
the gods lowered their heads
    to the top of their knees,
    and onto their princely seats.
Baal rebuked them:

"Gods, why have you lowered your heads
    to the top of your knees,
    and onto your princely seats?
I see, gods, that you are stricken
    with fear of the messengers of Sea,
    the mission of Judge River.
Gods, raise your heads
    from the top of your knees,
    from your princely seats.
For I will reply to the messengers of Sea,
    the mission of Judge River."
The gods raised their heads
    from the top of their knees,
    from their princely seats.
Then the messengers of Sea arrived,
    the mission of Judge River.
They did not fall at El's feet,
    they did not prostrate themselves before the Assembly
        in council;
still standing they spoke their speech,
    they repeated their message.
They seemed like one fire, or two;
    their tongues were sharpened swords.
They addressed the Bull, his father El:
"Message of Sea, your master,
    your lord, Judge River:
El, give up the one you are hiding,
    the one the masses are hiding;
give up Baal and his powers,
    the son of Dagon: I will assume his inheritance."
And the Bull, his father El, replied:
"Sea, Baal is your servant;
    River, Baal is your servant,
    the son of Dagon your prisoner.
He will be brought as your tribute,
    when the gods bring you payment,

and the holy ones gifts.
Then Baal will be gentle . . . ."
. . . .
"The mighty will fall to the ground,
    the powerful into the Slime."
These words had just come from her mouth,
    this speech from her lips,
she had just spoken,
        when he groaned from under Prince Sea's throne.
And Kothar-wa-Hasis replied:
"Let me tell you, Prince Baal,
    let me repeat, Rider on the Clouds:
behold, your enemy, Baal,
        behold, you will kill your enemy,
        behold, you will annihilate your foes.
You will take your eternal kingship,
    your dominion forever and ever."
Kothar brought down two clubs,
    and he pronounced their names:
"As for you, your name is Driver;
Driver, drive Sea,
    drive Sea from his throne,
    River from the seat of his dominion.
Dance in Baal's hands,
    like a vulture from his fingers.
Strike Prince Sea on the shoulder,
    Judge River between the arms."
The club danced in Baal's hands,
    like a vulture from his fingers.
It struck Prince Sea on the shoulder,
    Judge River between the arms.
Sea was strong; he did not sink;
    his joints did not shake;
    his frame did not collapse.
Kothar brought down two clubs,
    and he pronounced their names:

"As for you, your name is Chaser;
Chaser, chase Sea,
    chase Sea from his throne,
    River from the seat of his dominion.
Dance in Baal's hands,
    like a vulture from his fingers.
Strike Prince Sea on the skull,
    Judge River between the eyes.
Sea will stumble,
    he will fall to the ground."
And the club danced in Baal's hands,
    like a vulture from his fingers.
It struck Prince Sea on the skull,
    Judge River between the eyes.
Sea stumbled;
    he fell to the ground;
his joints shook;
    his frame collapsed.
Baal captured and drank Sea;
    he finished off Judge River.
Astarte shouted Baal's name:
"Hail, Baal the Conqueror!
    hail, Rider on the Clouds!
For Prince Sea is our captive,
    Judge River is our captive."

. . . .

II

. . . .

He served Baal the Conqueror,
    he honored the Prince, the Lord of the Earth:
he arose, prepared food, and gave it to him to eat;
    he carved a breast before him,
    with a sharp knife the loin of a fatling;
he got up, made ready the feast, and gave him drinks;

    he put a cup in his hand,
      a goblet in both his hands,
a large beaker, manifestly great,
    a jar to astound a mortal,
a holy cup which women should not see,
      a goblet which Asherah must not set her eye on;
he took a thousand jugs of wine,
    he mixed ten thousand in the mixing bowl.
He arose, he sang a song;
    there were cymbals in the minstrel's hands;
the Hero sang with a sweet voice
    of Baal on the peaks of Zaphon.
Baal looked at his daughters,
    he set his eye on Pidray, maid of light,
    also on Tallay, maid of rain.

· ·

The gates of Anat's house were shut,
    and the lads met the lady of the mountain.
And then Anat went to battle in the valley,
    she fought between the two cities:
she killed the people of the coast,
    she annihilated the men of the east.
Heads rolled under her like balls,
    hands flew over her like locusts,
    the warriors' hands like swarms of grasshoppers.
She fastened the heads to her back,
    she tied the hands to her belt.
She plunged knee-deep into the soldiers' blood,
    up to her thighs in the warriors' gore;
with a staff she drove off her enemies,
    with the string of her bow her opponents.
And then Anat arrived at her house,
    the goddess reached her palace;
there, not satisfied with her battling in the valley,
    her fighting between the two cities,
she made the chairs into warriors,

    she made the tables into an army,
    the stools into heroes.
She battled violently, and looked,
    Anat fought, and saw:
her soul swelled with laughter,
    her heart was filled with joy,
    Anat's soul was exuberant,
as she plunged knee-deep into the soldiers' blood,
    up to her thighs in the warriors' gore,
until she was satisfied with her battling in the house,
    her fighting between the tables.
The soldiers' blood was wiped from the house,
    oil of peace was poured from a bowl.
The Virgin Anat washed her hands,
    the Mistress of the Peoples her fingers;
she washed the soldiers' blood from her hands,
    the warriors' gore from her fingers.
She made the chairs chairs again,
    the tables tables;
    she made the stools stools.
She drew water and washed,
    the heavens' dew, the earth's oil,
    the rain of the Rider on the Clouds,
dew which the heavens pour,
    rain which is poured from the stars.

. . . .

"For the love of Baal the Conqueror,
    the love of Pidray, maid of light,
    the desire of Tallay, maid of rain,
    the love of Arsay, maid of the floods.
So then, lads, enter:
at Anat's feet bow down and adore,
    prostrate yourselves, worship her,
and say to the Virgin Anat,
    repeat to the Mistress of the Peoples:
'Message of Baal the Conqueror,

the word of the Conqueror of Warriors:
Remove war from the earth,
   set love in the ground,
pour peace into the heart of the earth,
   rain down love on the heart of the fields.
Hasten! hurry! rush!
Run to me with your feet,
   race to me with your legs;
for I have a word to tell you,
   a story to recount to you:
the word of the tree and the charm of the stone,
   the whisper of the heavens to the earth,
   of the seas to the stars.
I understand the lightning which the heavens do not know,
   the word which men do not know,
   and earth's masses cannot understand.
Come, and I will reveal it:
in the midst of my mountain, the divine Zaphon,
   in the sanctuary, in the mountain of my inheritance,
   in the pleasant place, in the hill I have conquered.' "
As soon as Anat saw the gods,
   her feet shook,
   her back was as though shattered,
   her face broke out in sweat,
   her joints trembled,
   her vertebrae became weak.
She raised her voice and shouted:
   "Why have Gapn and Ugar come?
What enemy has risen against Baal,
   what foe against the Rider on the Clouds?
Didn't I demolish El's Darling, Sea?
   didn't I finish off the divine river, Rabbim?
   didn't I snare the Dragon?
I enveloped him,
   I demolished the Twisting Serpent,
   the seven-headed monster.

I demolished El's Darling, Desire,
    I annihilated the divine calf, the Rebel;
I demolished El's bitch, Fire,
    I finished off El's daughter, Zebub.
I battled for the silver,
    I took possession of the gold.
Has Baal been driven from the heights of Zaphon?
    have they driven him from his royal chair,
    from his dais, from the seat of his dominion?
What enemy has risen against Baal,
    what foe against the Rider on the Clouds?"
Then the lads replied as follows:
"No enemy has risen against Baal,
    no foe against the Rider on the Clouds.
'Message of Baal the Conqueror,
    the word of the Conqueror of Warriors:
Remove war from the earth,
    set love in the ground,
pour peace into the heart of the earth,
    rain down love on the heart of the fields.
Hasten! hurry! rush!
Run to me with your feet,
    race to me with your legs;
for I have a word to tell you,
    a story to recount to you:
the word of the tree and the charm of the stone,
    the word which men do not know,
    and earth's masses cannot understand:
the whisper of the heavens to the earth,
    of the seas to the stars.
I understand the lightning which the heavens do not know.
Come, and I will reveal it:
in the midst of my mountain, the divine Zaphon,
    in the sanctuary, in the mountain of my inheritance.' "
And the Virgin Anat replied,
    the Mistress of the Peoples answered:

"I will remove war from the earth,
 I will set love in the ground,
I will pour peace into the heart of the earth,
 I will rain down love on the heart of the fields. . . .
I will remove war from the earth,
 I will set love in the ground,
I will pour peace into the heart of the earth,
 I will rain down love on the heart of the fields.
And I have something else to tell you:
Go, go, divine powers;
 you are slow, but I am swift.
Is not my mountain far from El,
 my cave far from the gods?
Two fathoms under the earth's springs,
 three rods under the caves."
Then she headed toward Baal on the heights of Zaphon,
 a thousand fields, ten thousand acres at each step.
Baal saw his sister coming,
 his father's daughter approaching;
he dismissed his wives from his presence.
He put an ox before her,
 a fatling in front of her.
She drew water and washed,
 the heavens' dew, the earth's oil,
dew which the heavens pour,
 rain which is poured from the stars. . . .

. . . .

"But Baal has no house like the other gods',
 no court like Asherah's sons':
El's home, his son's shelter,
 Lady Asherah-of-the-Sea's home,
the home of Pidray, maid of light,
 the shelter of Tallay, maid of rain,
the home of Arsay, maid of the floods,
 the home of the beautiful brides."
And the Virgin Anat replied:

"My father, El the Bull, will answer me,
    he'll answer me . . . or else
    I'll push him to the ground like a lamb,
I'll make his gray hair run with blood,
    his gray beard with gore,
unless he gives Baal a house like the other gods',
    and courts like Asherah's sons'."
She stamped her feet and left the earth;
    then she headed toward El,
at the source of the two rivers,
    in the midst of the two seas' pools;
she opened El's tent and entered
    the shrine of the King, the Father of Time. . . .
And the Virgin Anat spoke:
"Don't rejoice in your well-built house,
    in your well-built house, El,
don't rejoice in the height of your palace:
    don't rely on them!
I'll smash your head,
    I'll make your gray hair run with blood,
    your gray beard with gore."
El replied from the seven rooms,
    from the eight enclosures:
"I know you, daughter, how gentle you can be;
    but there is no restraint among goddesses.
What do you want, Virgin Anat?"
And the Virgin Anat replied:
"Your decree is wise, El,
    your wisdom is eternal,
    a lucky life is your decree.
But our king is Baal the Conqueror,
    our judge, higher than all:
all of us must bear his chalice,
    all of us must bear his cup."
The Bull El, her father, shouted loudly,
    El the King who brought her into being;

Asherah and her sons shouted,
    the goddess and her pride of lions:
"But Baal has no house like the other gods',
    no court like Asherah's sons':
El's home, his son's shelter,
    Lady Asherah-of-the-Sea's home,
the home of Pidray, maid of light,
    the shelter of Tallay, maid of rain,
the home of Arsay, maid of the floods,
    the home of the beautiful brides."

. . . .

"Cross Byblos, cross Qaal,
    cross the islands on the far horizon;
proceed, Asherah's Fisherman;
    advance, Holy and Most Blessed One;
then head toward Egypt,
    the god of it all—
Kaphtor is his royal house,
    Egypt is the land of his inheritance—
a thousand fields, ten thousand acres at each step.
At Kothar's feet bow down and adore,
    prostrate yourself and worship him;
and speak to Kothar-wa-Hasis,
    repeat to the Clever Craftsman:
'Message of Baal the Conqueror . . . .' "

. . . .

III

. . . .

The Bull El, her father, shouted loudly,
    El the King, who brought her into being;
Asherah and her sons shouted,
    the goddess and her pride of lions:
"But Baal has no house like the other gods',
    no court like Asherah's sons':

El's home, his son's shelter,
    Lady Asherah-of-the-Sea's home,
the home of the beautiful brides,
    the home of Pidray, maid of light,
the shelter of Tallay, maid of rain,
    the home of Arsay, maid of the floods.
But I have something else to tell you:
give gifts to Lady Asherah-of-the-Sea,
    presents to the Mother of the Gods.
Have the Clever One go up to the bellows,
    have Hasis take the tongs in his hands;
have him cast silver, have him pour gold:
    have him cast a thousand bars of silver,
    have him cast ten thousand bars of gold.
Have him cast a canopy and a reclining couch,
    a divine dais worth twenty thousand,
a divine dais decorated with silver,
    laminated with a layer of gold;
a divine seat set on top of it;
    a divine stool covered with electrum;
divine sandals with straps
    which he has plated with gold;
a divine table filled with everything
    yielded by the earth's foundations;
a divine bowl with a handle shaped like a lamb,
    with a base like the land of Yaman,
    where there are tens of thousands of wild oxen."

. . . .

She took her spindle in her hand,
    she raised her spindle in her right hand;
she tore off the garment which covered her flesh;
    she threw her robe into the sea,
    her two garments into the river;
she put a pot on the fire,
    a caldron on top of the coals.
She implored the Bull, El the Compassionate,

she entreated the Creator of All.
Then she raised her eyes and looked:
Asherah saw Baal coming,
the Virgin Anat coming,
the Mistress of the Peoples approaching.
Her feet shook,
her back was as though shattered,
her face broke out in sweat,
her joints trembled,
her vertebrae became weak.
She raised her voice and shouted:
"Why has Baal the Conqueror arrived?
why has the Virgin Anat arrived?
Have my enemies killed my sons?
have they finished off my pride of lions?"
But when Asherah saw the gleam of the silver,
the gleam of the silver and the shine of the gold,
Lady Asherah-of-the-Sea was glad;
she called to her lad:
"Look at the marvelous gifts,
Lady Asherah-of-the-Sea's Fisherman:
take your net in your hand . . ."
. . . .
Baal the Conqueror answered,
the Rider on the Clouds replied:
". . . He arose and spat at me
in the midst of the Assembly of the gods.
Filth has been set on my table,
bilge in my drinking cup.
Baal hates two kinds of banquets,
the Rider on the Clouds hates three:
a shameful banquet,
a degrading banquet,
a banquet with wanton women.
But here there is shameful behavior,
and here there are wanton women."

After Baal the Conqueror had arrived,
 the Virgin Anat arrived;
she gave her gifts to Lady Asherah-of-the-Sea,
 she gave her presents to the Mother of the Gods.
But Lady Asherah-of-the-Sea said:
"Why do you give gifts to Lady Asherah-of-the-Sea,
 presents to the Mother of the Gods?
You should give gifts to the Bull, El the Compassionate,
 and presents to the Creator of All."
But the Virgin Anat replied:
"We give gifts to you, Lady Asherah-of-the-Sea,
 presents to the Mother of the Gods. . . ."
. . . .
And Lady Asherah-of-the-Sea replied:
"Listen, Holy and Most Blessed One,
 Lady Asherah-of-the-Sea's Fisherman:
saddle an ass, harness a donkey,
 attach the silver reins, the golden bridle,
 fasten the reins to my she-ass."
The Holy and Most Blessed One obeyed;
he saddled the ass, he harnessed the donkey,
 he attached the silver reins, the golden bridle,
 he fastened the reins to the she-ass.
The Holy and Most Blessed One lifted her in his arms,
 he put Asherah on the ass's back,
 on the splendid back of the donkey.
The Holy One began to lead,
 the Most Blessed One like a guiding star.
The Virgin Anat followed her,
 as Baal left for the heights of Zaphon.
Then Asherah headed toward El,
 at the source of the two rivers,
 in the midst of the two seas' pools.
She opened El's tent and entered
 the shrine of the King, the Father of Time.
At El's feet she bowed down and adored;

she prostrated herself and worshiped him.
As soon as El saw her,
    he opened his mouth and laughed;
he put his feet on a stool,
    his fingers danced with excitement;
he raised his voice and shouted:
"Why has Lady Asherah-of-the-Sea arrived?
    why has the Mother of the Gods come?
Are you hungry . . .
    or thirsty . . . ?
    have something to eat or drink:
eat some food from the table,
    drink some wine from the goblet,
    blood of the vine from the golden cup.
Or does El the King's passion excite you?
    does the love of the Bull arouse you?"
But Lady Asherah-of-the-Sea replied:
"Your decree is wise, El,
    your wisdom is eternal,
    a lucky life is your decree.
But Baal the Conqueror is our king,
    our judge, higher than all.
All of us must bear his chalice,
    all of us must bear his cup."
The Bull El, her father, shouted loudly,
    El the King, who brought her into being;
Asherah and her sons shouted,
    the goddess and her pride of lions:
"But Baal has no house like the other gods',
    no court like Asherah's sons':
El's home, his son's shelter,
    Lady Asherah-of-the-Sea's home,
the home of the beautiful brides,
    the home of Pidray, maid of light,
the shelter of Tallay, maid of rain,
    the home of Arsay, maid of the floods."

But El the Kind, the Compassionate, replied:
"Am I a servant, a power of Asherah?
    am I a servant, holding a trowel,
    or Asherah's brickmaker?
Let a house like the other gods' be built for Baal,
    a court like Asherah's sons'."
And Lady Asherah-of-the-Sea replied:
"You are great, El, you are truly wise;
    your gray beard truly instructs you . . . .
Now Baal will begin the rainy season,
    the season of wadis in flood;
and he will sound his voice in the clouds,
    flash his lightning to the earth.
Let him complete his house of cedar!
    let him construct his house of bricks!
Let Baal the Conqueror be commanded:
'Call a caravan into your house,
    a wagon train within your palace;
the mountains will bring you much silver,
    the hills fine gold in abundance;
    the camels will bring you jewels.
And build a house of silver and gold,
    a house of purest lapis lazuli.' "
The Virgin Anat was glad;
    she stamped her feet and left the earth;
then she headed toward Baal on the heights of Zaphon,
    a thousand fields, ten thousand acres at each step.
The Virgin Anat laughed;
    she raised her voice and shouted:
"I have good news for you, Baal:
a house like your brothers' will be built for you,
    and a court like your cousins';
call a caravan into your house,
    a wagon train within your palace;
the mountains will bring you much silver,
    the hills fine gold in abundance;

and build a house of silver and gold,
    a house of purest lapis lazuli."
Baal the Conqueror was glad;
he called a caravan into his house,
    a wagon train within his palace;
the mountains brought him much silver,
    the hills fine gold in abundance;
    the camels brought him jewels.
He sent messengers to Kothar-wa-Hasis.

Now go back to the passage "When the lads were sent."*

After Kothar-wa-Hasis had arrived,
    Baal put an ox before him,
    a fatling in front of him.
A chair was brought, and he was seated
    to the right of Baal the Conqueror.
When the god had eaten and drunk,
    Baal the Conqueror spoke,
    the Rider on the Clouds said:
"Kothar, hurry, build a house;
    hurry, erect a palace;
hurry, build a house;
    hurry, raise a palace
    among the peaks of Zaphon.
Let the house extend over a thousand fields,
    the palace over ten thousand acres."
And Kothar-wa-Hasis replied:
"Listen, Baal the Conqueror,
    pay attention, Rider on the Clouds:

---

*A note to the reader of the tablet to repeat a formulaic passage (now lost) describing the journey of Baal's messengers to Kothar-wa-Hasis, their delivery of the message, and Kothar's journey to Baal.

I should put a casement in the house,
    a window within the palace."
But Baal the Conqueror replied:
"Don't put a casement in the house,
    a window within the palace. . . ."
But Kothar-wa-Hasis replied:
"You'll recall my words, Baal."
And Kothar-wa-Hasis repeated:
"Listen, Baal the Conqueror:
I should put a casement in the house,
    a window within the palace."
But Baal the Conqueror replied:
"Don't put a casement in the house,
    a window within the palace. . . ."
But Kothar-wa-Hasis replied:
"You'll recall my words, Baal."
They built his house,
    they erected his palace;
they went to the Lebanon for wood,
    to Sirion for the finest cedar;
they went to the Lebanon for wood,
    to Sirion for the finest cedar.
They set fire to the house,
    they inflamed the palace.
One day passed, then two:
    the fire ate the house,
    the flames consumed the palace.
Three days passed, then four:
    the fire ate the house,
    the flames consumed the palace.
Five days passed, then six:
    the fire ate the house,
    the flames consumed the palace.
Then, on the seventh day,
    the fire died down in the house,
    the flames died down in the palace:

the silver had turned into blocks,
    the gold had become bricks.
Baal the Conqueror was glad:
"I have built my house of silver,
    my palace of gold."
Baal prepared the house,
    Hadad made preparations within his palace:
he slaughtered oxen,
    he killed sheep,
      bulls, fatling rams,
      yearling calves;
he strangled lambs and kids.
He invited his brothers into his house,
    his cousins within his palace;
    he invited Asherah's seventy sons.
He gave the gods lambs;
    he gave the gods ewes;
    he gave the gods oxen;
    he gave the gods cows;
    he gave the gods seats;
    he gave the gods thrones;
he gave the gods a jar of wine;
    he gave the goddesses a cask of wine.
Until the gods had eaten and drunk their fill,
    he gave them sucklings to eat,
    with a sharp knife carved the breast of a fatling.
They drank wine from goblets,
    blood of the vine from golden cups.

. . . .

Baal captured sixty-six cities,
    seventy-seven towns;
Baal sacked eighty,
    Baal sacked ninety;
then Baal returned to his house.
And Baal the Conqueror said:
"I will do it, Kothar, Sea's son,

Kothar, son of the Assembly:
let a window be opened in the house,
 a casement within the palace;
then a slit can be opened in the clouds,
 as Kothar-wa-Hasis said."
Kothar-wa-Hasis laughed;
 he raised his voice and shouted:
"Baal the Conqueror, didn't I tell you:
 'You'll recall my words, Baal'?"
He opened a window in the house,
 a casement within the palace.
Then Baal opened a slit in the clouds,
 Baal sounded his holy voice,
 Baal thundered from his lips . . .
the earth's high places shook.
Baal's enemies fled to the woods,
 Hadad's haters took to the mountains.
And Baal the Conqueror said:
"Hadad's enemies, why are you quaking?
 why are you quaking, assailers of the Valiant One?"
Baal's eye guided his hand,
 as he swung a cedar in his right hand.
So Baal was enthroned in his house.
"No other king or non-king
 shall set his power over the earth.
I will send no tribute to El's son Death,
 no homage to El's Darling, the Hero.
Let Death cry to himself,
 let the Darling grumble in his heart;
for I alone will rule over the gods;
 I alone will fatten gods and men;
 I alone will satisfy earth's masses."
Baal called to his lads:
"Look, Gapn and Ugar, sons of Galmat . . . .
. . . .
Then head toward Mount Targuziza,

  toward Mount Tharumagi,
  toward the mounds that block the way to the
   underworld.
Raise the mountain with your hands,
  the hill on top of your palms;
then go down to the sanatorium of the underworld;
  you will be counted among those who go down into the
   earth.
Then head toward the midst of his city, the Swamp,
  Muck, his royal house,
  Phlegm, the land of his inheritance.
But, divine powers, be on your guard:
  don't approach El's son, Death,
lest he put you in his mouth like a lamb,
  crush you like a kid in his jaws.
Sun, the gods' torch, burns,
  the heavens shimmer under the sway of El's Darling,
   Death.
A thousand fields, ten thousand acres at each step;
  at Death's feet bow down and adore,
  prostrate yourselves and worship him;
and speak to El's son, Death,
  repeat to El's Darling, the Hero:
Message of Baal the Conqueror,
  the word of the Conqueror of Warriors:
'I have built my house of silver,
  my palace of gold. . . .' "

. . . .

IV

"When you killed Lotan, the Fleeing Serpent,
  finished off the Twisting Serpent,
  the seven-headed monster,
the heavens withered and drooped
  like the folds of your robes . . . .

Now you will surely descend into the throat of El's son,
    Death,
    into the watery depths of El's Darling, the Hero."
The gods left; they did not turn back;
    they headed toward Baal on the heights of Zaphon;
then Gapn and Ugar spoke:
"Message of El's son, Death,
    the word of El's Darling, the Hero:
'My appetite is like that of a lioness,
    or the desire of a dolphin in the sea;
my pool seizes the wild oxen,
    my well grabs the deer;
when I have the appetite for an ass,
    then I eat with both my hands. . . ."

. . . .
"One lip to the earth, one lip to the heavens;
    he will stretch his tongue to the stars.
Baal must enter inside him;
    he must go down into his mouth,
like an olive cake,
    the earth's produce,
    the fruit of the trees."
Baal the Conqueror became afraid;
    the Rider on the Clouds was terrified:
"Leave me; speak to El's son Death,
    repeat to El's Darling, the Hero:
'Message of Baal the Conqueror,
    the word of the Conqueror of Warriors:
Hail, El's son Death!
    I am your servant, I am yours forever.' "
They left; they did not turn back;
    then they headed toward El's son Death,
to the midst of his city, the Swamp,
    Muck, his royal house,
    Phlègm, the land of his inheritance.
They raised their voices and shouted:

" 'Message of Baal the Conqueror,
    the word of the Conqueror of Warriors:
Hail, El's son Death!
    I am your servant, I am yours forever.' "
El's son Death was glad . . .

· ·

". . . I will put him into the hole of the gods of the earth.
As for you, take your clouds,
    your wind, your bolts, your rain;
take with you your seven lads,
    your eight noble boars;
take with you Pidray, maid of light;
    take with you Tallay, maid of rain;
then head toward Mount Kankaniya:.
raise the mountain with your hands,
    the hill on top of your palms;
then go down to the sanatorium of the underworld;
    you will be counted among those who go down into the
        earth.
And the gods will know that you have died."
Baal the Conqueror obeyed.
He fell in love with a heifer in the desert pasture,
    a young cow in the fields on Death's shore:
he slept with her seventy-seven times,
    he mounted her eighty-eight times;
and she became pregnant,
    and she bore him the Lord.

· ·

"We arrived at the pleasant place, the desert pasture,
    at the lovely fields on Death's shore.
We came upon Baal:
    he had fallen to the ground.
Baal the Conqueror has died;
    the Prince, the Lord of the Earth, has perished."
Then El the Kind, the Compassionate,
    came down from his throne,

      sat on his stool,
and coming down from his stool he sat on the ground.
He poured earth on his head as a sign of mourning,
      on his skull the dust in which he rolled;
      he covered his loins with sackcloth.
He cut his skin with a knife,
      he made incisions with a razor;
he cut his cheeks and chin,
      he raked his arms with a reed,
he plowed his chest like a garden,
      he raked his back like a valley.
He raised his voice and shouted:
"Baal is dead: what will happen to the peoples?
      Dagon's son: what will happen to the masses?
      I will go down into the earth in Baal's place."
Anat also was taking a walk and wandering
      on every mountain in the heart of the earth,
      on every hill in the heart of the fields.
She arrived at the pleasant place, the desert pasture,
      the lovely fields on Death's shore.
She came upon Baal:
      he had fallen to the ground.
She covered her loins with sackcloth.

V

She cut her skin with a knife,
      she made incisions with a razor;
she cut her cheeks and chin,
      she raked her arms with a reed,
she plowed her chest like a garden,
      she raked her back like a valley.
"Baal is dead: what will happen to the peoples?
      Dagon's son: what will happen to the masses?
      Let us go down into the earth in Baal's place."

Sun, the gods' torch, went down with her.
When she had finished weeping,
    had drunk her tears like wine,
she called to Sun, the gods' torch:
    "Lift Baal the Conqueror onto me!"
Sun, the gods' torch, obeyed;
    she lifted up Baal the Conqueror;
    she put him on Anat's shoulders.
She brought him up to the peaks of Zaphon;
    she wept for him and buried him;
    she put him into the hole of the gods of the earth.
She slaughtered seventy wild oxen
    as an oblation for Baal the Conqueror.
She slaughtered seventy plow oxen
    as an oblation for Baal the Conqueror.
She slaughtered seventy sheep
    as an oblation for Baal the Conqueror.
She slaughtered seventy deer
    as an oblation for Baal the Conqueror.
She slaughtered seventy mountain goats
    as an oblation for Baal the Conqueror.
She slaughtered seventy asses
    as an oblation for Baal the Conqueror. . . .
Then she headed toward El
    at the source of the two rivers,
    in the midst of the two seas' pools.
She opened El's tent and entered
    the shrine of the King, the Father of Time.
At El's feet she bowed down and adored,
    she prostrated herself and worshiped him.
She raised her voice and shouted:
"Now let Asherah and her sons rejoice,
    the goddess and her pride of lions:
for Baal the Conqueror has died,
    the Prince, the Lord of the Earth, has perished."
El called to Lady Asherah-of-the-Sea:

"Listen, Lady Asherah-of-the-Sea:
give me one of your sons;
    I'll make him king."
And Lady Asherah-of-the-Sea replied:
    "Why not make Yadi-Yalhan king?"
But El the Kind, the Compassionate, replied:
"He's much too weak to race,
    to compete in spear-throwing with Baal,
    with Dagon's son in contest."
And Lady Asherah-of-the-Sea replied:
"Can't we make Athtar the Awesome king?
    Let Athtar the Awesome be king!"
Then Athtar the Awesome
    went up to the peaks of Zaphon;
he sat on Baal the Conqueror's throne:
    his feet did not reach the footstool,
    his head did not reach the headrest.
And Athtar the Awesome spoke:
    "I can't be king on the peaks of Zaphon."
Athtar the Awesome descended,
    he descended from Baal the Conqueror's throne,
    and he became king of the underworld, the god of it all.

. . . .

One day passed, then two;
    and the Maiden Anat approached him.
Like the heart of a cow for her calf,
    like the heart of a ewe for her lamb,
    so was Anat's heart for Baal.
She seized Death by the edge of his clothes,
    she grabbed him by the hem of his garments;
she raised her voice and shouted:
    "Come, Death, give me my brother!"
And El's son Death replied:
    "What do you want, Virgin Anat?
I was taking a walk and wandering
    on every mountain in the heart of the earth,

on every hill in the heart of the fields;
I felt a desire for human beings,
    a desire for earth's masses.
I arrived at my pleasant place, the desert pasture,
    the lovely fields on Death's shore.
I approached Baal the Conqueror;
    I put him in my mouth like a lamb,
    he was crushed like a kid in my jaws."
Sun, the gods' torch, burned;
    the heavens shimmered under the sway of El's son
      Death.
One day passed, then two;
    the days became months.
    The Maiden Anat approached him.
Like the heart of a cow for her calf,
    like the heart of a ewe for her lamb,
    so was Anat's heart for Baal.
She seized El's son Death:
    with a sword she split him;
    with a sieve she winnowed him;
    with fire she burned him;
    with a hand mill she ground him;
    in the fields she sowed him.
"May the birds not eat his remains,
    may the fowl not consume his parts:
    let flesh cry out to flesh!"

. . . .

"And if Baal the Conqueror lives,
    if the Prince, the Lord of the Earth, has revived,
in a dream of El the Kind, the Compassionate,
    in a vision of the Creator of All,
let the heavens rain down oil,
    let the wadis run with honey;
then I will know that Baal the Conqueror lives,
    that the Prince, the Lord of the Earth, has revived."
In a dream of El the Kind, the Compassionate,

    in a vision of the Creator of All,
the heavens rained down oil,
    the wadis ran with honey.
El the Kind, the Compassionate, was glad:
    he put his feet on a stool,
    he opened his mouth and laughed;
he raised his voice and shouted:
"Now I can sit back and relax;
    my heart inside me can relax;
for Baal the Conqueror lives,
    the Prince, the Lord of the Earth, has revived."
El called to the Virgin Anat:
"Listen, Virgin Anat—
    speak to Sun, the gods' torch:
'Sun, the furrows in the fields have dried,
    the furrows in El's fields have dried;
    Baal has neglected the furrows of his plowland.
Where is Baal the Conqueror?
    where is the Prince, the Lord of the Earth?' "
The Virgin Anat left;
    she headed toward Sun, the gods' torch;
she raised her voice and shouted:
"Message of the Bull, El your father,
    the word of the Kind One, your parent:
'Sun, the furrows in the fields have dried,
    the furrows in El's fields have dried;
    Baal has neglected the furrows of his plowland.
Where is Baal the Conqueror?
    where is the Prince, the Lord of the Earth?' "
And Sun, the gods' torch, replied:
"Pour sparkling wine from its container,
    bring a garland for your relative;
    and I will look for Baal the Conqueror."
And the Virgin Anat replied:
"Wherever you go, Sun,
    wherever you go, may El protect you."

. . . .
Baal seized Asherah's sons;
    he struck Rabbim on the shoulder;
    he struck the Waves with his club;
he pushed sallow Death to the ground.
Baal returned to his royal chair,
    to his dais, the seat of his dominion.
The days became months,
    the months became years.
Then, in the seventh year,
    El's son Death spoke to Baal the Conqueror;
    he raised his voice and shouted:
"Baal, because of you I suffered shame;
    because of you I suffered splitting with a sword;
    because of you I suffered burning with fire;
    because of you I suffered grinding with a hand mill;
    because of you I suffered winnowing with a sieve;
    because of you I suffered scattering in the fields;
    because of you I suffered sowing in the sea.
Give me one of your brothers,
    so that I may sit down and eat. . . ."
. . . .
"Let Baal give his little brothers for me to eat,
    his mother's sons for me to consume."
He returned to Baal on the peaks of Zaphon;
    he raised his voice and shouted:
"Let Baal give his little brothers for me to eat,
    his mother's sons for me to consume."
They butted each other like camels—
    Death was strong, Baal was strong.
They gored each other like wild oxen—
    Death was strong, Baal was strong.
They bit each other like serpents—
    Death was strong, Baal was strong.
They kicked each other like stallions—
    Death fell, Baal fell.

Sun shouted from above:
"Listen, El's son Death:
how can you battle with Baal the Conqueror?
    how can you keep the Bull, El your father, from
      hearing you?
He will surely undermine the foundations of your throne;
    he will surely overturn your royal chair;
    he will surely smash your scepter of judgment."
El's son Death became fearful;
    El's Darling, the Hero, was terrified;
    Death was afraid of her voice.

. . . .

"But you will eat the sacrificial meal,
    you will drink the offertory wine."
Sun judged the Healers,
    Sun judged the divine ones:
"Gods, Death is yours,
    Kothar, your friend, is yours,
    and your acquaintance Hasis.
In Sea—Desire and the Dragon—
    Kothar-wa-Hasis wandered,
    Kothar-wa-Hasis roamed.

The scribe was Ilimilku from Shubbani;
the reciter was Attanu-Purlianni, the chief priest,
    the chief herdsman;
the sponsor was Niqmaddu, king of Ugarit, master of
      Yargub,
    lord of Tharumani.

GLOSSARY
OF NAMES

Abiluma   City near which Aqhat was killed; its patron was the moon god.

Anat   The "violent goddess," goddess of love and of war. She is the wife and sister of Baal, and often appears in winged form. Her title "the Virgin" is not literal, but indicates her perennial nubility; she is also called "the Maiden" and "Mistress of the Peoples."

Aqhat   The son of Danel, with whom he shares the epithet "the Hero." He is killed at the instigation of Anat.

Arsay   A daughter of Baal. Her name means "earthy"; the translation of her title "maid of the floods" is not certain.

Asherah   El's wife and the principal goddess of Sidon and Tyre. She is closely related to and sometimes identified with Astarte. She is the "Mother of the Gods"; her name was originally pronounced Athirat, and in its full form means "she treads on Sea."

Assembly   The council of the gods, over which El presided.

Astarte   Like Anat, a goddess of love and war. She is closely related to Baal, as her title "Baal's other self" (literally "name of Baal") shows.

Athtar the Awesome   The deified morning star and son of Asherah who attempts to replace Baal; after his failure he is made a ruler in the underworld.

Baal   The Canaanite storm god, as indicated by his epithet "the Rider on the Clouds." He is the central deity in most of the surviving myths, probably because of his role as fertility god: he is the son of Dagon (god of grain) and, as god of the storm whose voice is thunder, he provides the essential rain which restores vegetation to the earth; thus he is called "Healer." His other titles include "the Prince," "the Conqueror (of Warriors)," and "the Lord of the Earth"; he is also called "Hadad." Baal corresponds to the gods Marduk in Babylon and Zeus in Greece.

Bit-Hubur   *See* Hubur.

Byblos   A Canaanite city on the coast of Lebanon north of Beirut.

Chaser One of Baal's clubs made by Kothar-wa-Hasis.

Clever Craftsman A title of Kothar-wa-Hasis.

Council of El The Assembly of the gods.

Dagon Baal's father; his name means "grain," and was originally pronounced Dagan. Although he has no major role in the surviving stories, he was an important deity at Ugarit.

Danataya The wife of Danel.

Danel The father of Aqhat and Pagat and the husband of Danataya. His patron god is apparently Baal, as his epithet "the Healer's man" suggests. The appellation "the Hero" is an indication of noble birth, and Danel was the king of his city-state.

Death The god of death, pestilence, and plague, who rules the underworld. In *Baal* he temporarily gains control over the storm god.

Desire An enemy of Baal whom Anat claims to have killed; perhaps an aspect of Sea.

Ditan Kirta's clan.

Dragon A manifestation of Sea.

Driver One of Baal's clubs made by Kothar-wa-Hasis.

El The head of the Semitic pantheon and the father of gods and mortals, corresponding to Greek Kronos and Mesopotamian Anu. His epithets describe him: "the Bull," "the Father of Time," "the King," "the Creator of All," "the Kind, the Compassionate," "the Holy One."

El's Darling A title of Death, of Sea, and of Desire.

Father of Men A title of El.

Fire "El's bitch"; an enemy of Baal whom Anat claims to have killed.

Fisherman A divine attendant of Lady Asherah-of-the-Sea.

Galmat Mother of Gapn and Ugar; her name probably means "darkness."

Gapn One of Baal's messengers, always mentioned with Ugar. Their names mean "vineyard" and "field," respectively, reflecting Baal's role as fertility god.

Gatherers of Ditan The divinized ancestors of Kirta's clan.

Hadad A name of Baal, meaning "the thunderer."

Harnam A city in northeastern Lebanon (modern Hermel) whose patron god was Baal.

Hasis *See* Kothar-wa-Hasis.

Healer A title of Baal, referring to an aspect of his role as god of fertility and Danel's patron.

Healers   Gods of the underworld, probably deified ancestors who promoted the well-being of their families.

Hero   A title indicating nobility applied to Aqhat, Danel, Death, and Ilihu.

Hirgab   The father of vultures.

Holy and Most Blessed One   A title of Lady Asherah-of-the-Sea's Fisherman.

Horon   A god, probably of the underworld, and perhaps a son of Astarte.

Hubur   The capital city of Kirta's kingdom; also called Bit-Hubur ("house of Hubur").

Hurriya   The daughter of Pabil and the wife of Kirta.

Ilihu   A son of Kirta and brother of Thitmanit.

Ilisha   The carpenter god, perhaps to be identified with Kothar-wa-Hasis.

Judge River   A title of Sea; "judge" in Ugaritic, as also occasionally in the Bible, means "ruler." The sea was thought of as a river which encircled the earth.

Kaphtor   An ancient name for Crete, and one of the homes of Kothar-wa-Hasis.

Kind (and Holy) One   A title of El.

Kirta   King of Hubur and hero of the mythic cycle named after him. He was of divine parentage, and was the father of Ilihu, Thitmanit, and Yassib by his wife, the Lady Hurriya. He is called "the Gracious One," "the Noble," "the Lad of El."

Kothar-wa-Hasis   The craftsman of the gods; his name means "skillful and wise." Like his Greek counterpart Hephaistos, he builds the gods' dwellings and makes their weapons. As "lord of Egypt" he was probably identified with the Egyptian god Ptah. His other titles include "the Clever One," "the Handcraftsman," "son of Sea," and "son of the Assembly."

Lebanon   The westernmost of the two mountain ranges that run from north to south through modern Syria and Lebanon. The range was often snow-covered; this is the origin of its name, which means "white."

Lotan   One of Baal's enemies, probably a manifestation of Sea, who is called Leviathan in the Bible.

Mararat-tagullal-banir   City near which Aqhat was killed; the meaning and vocalization of the name are uncertain.

Mistress of the Peoples   A title of Anat.

Most High   A title of Baal.

Mount Kankaniya   A mountain at the entrance to the underworld.

Mount Targuziza   A mountain at the entrance to the underworld.

Mount Tharumagi   A mountain at the entrance to the underworld.

Muck   A name for the underworld.

Pabil   King of Udm and father of Hurriya.

Pagat   Danel's daughter and Aqhat's sister, who avenges the latter's death. Her name means "girl."

Phlegm   A name for the underworld.

Pidray   A daughter of Baal, called "maid of light." Her name means "misty" or "cloudy."

Prince   A title of Baal.

Prince Moon   The Canaanite moon god and patron of the city Abiluma.

Qaal   A place whose location is unknown.

Qor-maym   City near which Aqhat was killed; its name means "source of water."

Rabbim   A title of Sea, meaning "the many." Compare the biblical phrase "the many (or the mighty) waters."

Rebel   The divine calf; an enemy of Baal whom Anat claimed to have killed.

Resheph   God of plague; his name means "flame."

River   *See* Judge River.

Samal   The mother of vultures.

Sea   The god of the sea and one of Baal's adversaries. Sea appears in various forms that seem to be personified monsters; these include "the Dragon," "Lotan," "Rabbim," and "the Waves." Like Baal's other adversary, Death, Sea is called El's Darling.

Serpent   One of Baal's enemies, and probably a manifestation of Sea; compare Revelation 12:9.

Shataqat   Goddess of healing; her name means "she caused (disease) to pass away."

Singers   A title of the Wise Women, probably reflecting their use of incantations.

Sirion   The mountain range east of the Lebanon, called by modern geographers the Anti-Lebanon.

Slime   A name for the underworld.

Sun   The Canaanite goddess Shapash (or Shapshu), called "the gods' torch."

Swallows   An unexplained designation of the Wise Women.

Swamp A name for the underworld.

Tallay A daughter of Baal. Her name means "dewy" and she is called "maid of rain."

Ten Thousand The deified stars.

Thitmanit The eighth daughter of Kirta, and Ilihu's sister; her name means "eighth."

Twisting Serpent A manifestation of Sea.

Udm The capital city of Pabil's kingdom.

Ugar *See* Gapn.

Valiant One A title of Baal.

Waves A manifestation of Sea.

Wise Women Seven goddesses who presided over marriage and child-birth. Their names suggest a relationship to Kothar-wa-Hasis.

Yadi-Yalhan One of Asherah's sons; his name means "he knows how to serve."

Yaman A place whose location is unknown.

Yassib A son of Kirta.

Yatpan Anat's henchman, "the Lady's man," and Aqhat's killer.

Zaphon The mountain on which Baal lives, located north of Ras Shamra at the mouth of the Orontes River, near the present border between Turkey and Syria.

Zebub El's daughter and an enemy of Baal whom Anat claims to have killed; her name may mean "fly," as in the phrase "lord of the flies."